How to Organize and Run A Successful Classroom

H.I.P. TIPS

A GUIDE FOR ELEMENTARY TEACHERS

by Bonnie Williamson

Dynamic Teaching Company
2247 Palmwood Ct.
Rancho Cordova, CA. 95670

H.I.P. TIPS
How To Organize And Run A Successful
Classroom: A Guide For Elementary Teachers
By Bonnie Williamson

Published by:
Dynamic Teaching Company
2247 Palmwood Court
Rancho Cordova, CA 95670, U.S.A.

Copyright © 1986 by Bonnie Williamson
First Printing 1986

Printed in the United States of America

Illustrations and cover design by William Boddy

Library of Congress Cataloging in Publication Data.
Williamson, Bonnie
    H.I.P. TIPS
    How To Organize And Run a Successful Classroom:
    A Guide For Elementary Teachers
    Includes Appendix-Resources

Library of Congress Catalog Number 86-71336

ISBN: 0-937899-04-6

*To Marie Van Dyke who took
the time to teach me the "HIP way".*

Contents

Introduction

Mary Ann is a first year teacher. Her room of 32 fourth graders abounds with students who constantly misbehave. She's not sure she can stick out the year.

Tony has taught for nine years. He has used several different types of discipline programs in his classroom with so-so success. This coming September he plans on moving from the intermediate segment to primary and he wants to find a new classroom management system — one that works.

Linda has 15 years' experience. She teaches first grade and is tired of her room arranged in the traditional manner with six straight rows of desks. She says, "I would like to experiment just a little and change my room around."

Here are three teachers who are seeking a better way to manage their classrooms.

How To Organize And Run A Successful Classroom is a step-by-step guide demonstrating how to use the Honor Incentive Program (HIP). In this book Mary Ann, Tony and Linda will discover how to plan and conduct a HIP classroom. The book is a classroom recipe book, if you will, to guide, give tips and point the way to success in classroom management.

The HIP system provides teachers with the power to get students to do what the teacher wants them to do. Yet HIP is not a dictatorial management style but rather a democratic process of classroom involvement between teacher and students.

Elections are held, jobs gained through the voting process and discipline maintained through peer pressure, leaving the teacher to do what he or she does best — teach!

It has been exciting to field test HIP these past two years and now to see the procedure come to life in this book. I am confident that those who read and apply these techniques in their own rooms will see positive changes.

Acknowledgements

First, I thank Lynn Pribus for her patient help and continual encouragement in editing the book. She reinforced for me the positive motivating effect of "earning points."

I also thank teacher Donna Allen for her helpful suggestions during the final phase of the project.

A big thanks also to students and parents who rallied behind me as I field tested HIP the past two years in my classroom.

CHAPTER 1

THE
HONOR INCENTIVE POINT
SYSTEM

THE IDEA!!

1

The Honor Incentive
Point System

*W*hether you are 21 or 51, a beginning teacher or one who has taught 30 years, sooner or later, I predict, you will ask, "what can I do so I can teach more and discipline less?"

During my 20 years in the classroom, after trying a number of different discipline methods with my students, reading many management books and attending workshops, I was still not fully satisfied with the results.

This year, however, things were different. My second graders took top honors in the Science Fair, had their names printed in local newspapers for the unusual number of library books read and frequently received a trophy in the cafeteria for good behavior.

I was also rewarded. I received my highest teacher evaluation ever, excellent in every area of my teaching and classroom management. My classroom became the school's "showplace" for exhibiting excellence in education to student teachers, substitutes, and inquiring parents.

What was my secret? I used a classroom management system I learned from Marie Van Dyke, a remarkable 30-year veteran of the elementary school classroom. Mrs. Van Dyke attended San Francisco State College in the mid-40s as an elementary education major. During her final year in college, she was selected by a committee to be a student teacher at Peralta School — a prestigious teacher training institution in Oakland, California. Many of her classroom management and organization skills came from Peralta and her supervisors there. Through the years she has added her own ideas developing her successful Honor Incentive Point (HIP) system approach to classroom management.

Today parents ask to have their child in Mrs. Van Dyke's primary room while the youngster is still in nursery school and student teachers are eager to be placed in her room because of her reputation as an outstanding teacher and disciplinarian.

Eighteen months ago, I selected Mrs. Van Dyke to be my personal HIP mentor teacher. I visited her classroom and took notes as she marked points on the chalkboard, conducted Class Meetings, and presided over the Job Meeting (all part of the HIP system), and we spent hours talking about her successful HIP classroom.

I then used the HIP system in my own room. Along with the system, I incorporated a number of my own successful teaching techniques. Many of these ideas appear in the next 11 chapters as HIP TIPS. From this educational mix came this book on how to successfully teach in a HIP classroom.

Why does this method work? What is the secret? Simply the system is an effective, workable partnership between the teacher and students.

Peer persuasion, rather than teacher coercion is the main focus of HIP. The teacher serves as Director of the Board and also, at times, as a judge but mostly as a supportive leader in the classroom. The system works because it allows you, the teacher, to join with students in a *shared* responsibility for a classroom where learning takes place.

HIP is built around a weekly job incentive program, specific classroom rules, daily Class Meetings and a weekly Honor Point chart.

The HIP system is simple, yet well planned and most of all *it works.* In the next chapter you will learn how to arrange your classroom to have a successful school year.

CHAPTER 2

GET READY, GET SET, GO!

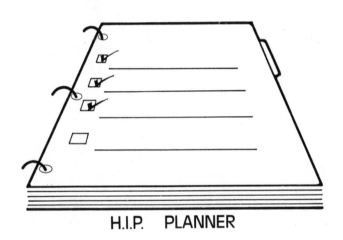

H.I.P.   PLANNER

2

Get Ready . . . Get Set . . . Go!

*D*uring the spring, many schools hold what they call a "Play Day" or "Field Day." Students look forward to this release from the classroom with joyful glee while many teachers pray the day will soon be over!

Still most of these Play Days turn out to be resoundingly successful. Why? Because hours of preparation have gone into planning the activities, soliciting parent volunteers and getting the equipment organized.

It's every bit as essential to be well organized in the classroom and rather than planning for one day you must have overall goals and planning for the entire year. You must preplan for success. How do you begin to do this?

ROOM ARRANGEMENT

The HIP system is based upon arranging the room into "stations." A station is a group of desks placed together and for my example I'm using 33 desks divided into three stations.

Here's how it would work. Arrange the three stations around the shape of a "U". On the left side of the "U" place five desks spaced at least 12 inches apart. Behind these, stagger six desks so each student in the back row has a clear view of the front of the room. Or, if space in back is a problem, place six desks in front and five in back. (See drawing on page 9.)

Repeat the arrangement with 11 more desks at the "bottom" of the "U", then move on to the right hand side of the "U" and space the remaining 11 desks.

Place your own desk in front of the room to one side. Be sure to position it to provide an unobstructed view of you and the chalkboard.

CHAIRMAN OF THE BOARD

In big corporations one room is designated "The Board Room." Instead of having your board members seated around the table they are spaced around the outside of the "U".

As teacher, or chairman of the 33 member board, you need a special table which will be as important to you in the next ten months as to any Chairman of the Board.

Ask your principal for a rectangular table about six feet long and three feet wide. Place the table lengthwise in the center of the "U" with your own special chair at the head of the table about three to four feet away from the chalkboard, which is behind you. (See drawing on page 10.)

THE CHAIRMAN'S ACCESSORIES

Not only must a chairman have a table but also accessories to make meetings run smoothly such as pen, pad and perhaps a gavel to gain attention. You, too, need specific items nearby to make the day pass in an orderly manner for you and for your students.

There are several ways to gain students' attention, such as ringing a bell, standing with one arm raised or sounding a note on a

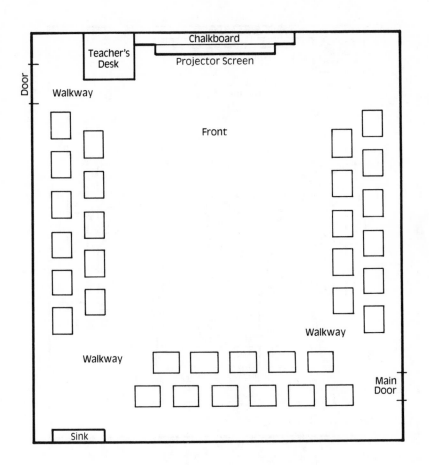

HIP STATION ARRANGEMENT

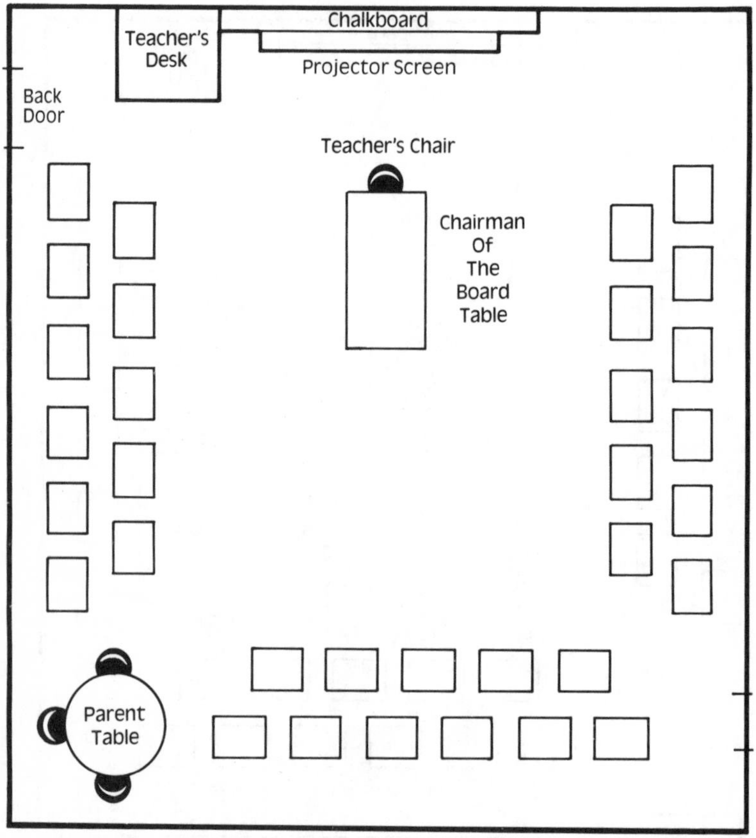

Chalkboard

Teacher's Desk

Projector Screen

Back Door

Teacher's Chair

Chairman Of The Board Table

Parent Table

**CHAIRMAN OF THE BOARD
TABLE**

piano if such an instrument is available. A small bell with a melodic sound works particularly well.

It is also important to make the room colorful and attractive. Pick out a bright place mat and put it in the middle of the table. Add three baskets and a colorful coffee mug or jar. The baskets and mug are placed on the mat. Keep a fresh supply of sharpened pencils in the mug. In one large basket students place broken pencils before taking a fresh pencil. In another basket (pick a different color) keep a supply of crayons, erasers or whatever extra items you want to have available for those with missing supplies.

The third basket holds slips of paper for jotting messages, ballots for voting and for writing out the correct spelling words for students, as needed.

HIP TIP By keeping supplies such as pencils, crayons and erasers on the "Chairman of the Board" table, you cut out many potential behavior problems. When supplies are in the back of the room, you set up students to loiter, fight over the longest pencil and spend valuable minutes digging through a bucket of supplies looking for the "perfect eraser" while missing an entire spelling test.

Depending on how you operate your room, you may keep your lesson plans on your regular desk or on your table. Since you will spend more of your day at the table, keeping the lesson plans on the table can save minutes and footwork.

PARENT TABLE

When parents take the time from their busy schedule to come and help in the classroom it is important to create an area where they can sit quietly and observe the classroom, grade papers or listen to students read aloud. Find a sturdy table and several chairs which can be placed in the back of the room for their use. If you cannot locate such a table at school, look around at garage sales for something suitable at a fair price.

Now that you have your room arranged, you will discover how important written rules and oral directions are. You are going to find how YOU can run a successful room.

CHAPTER 3

THE 5 BIG RULES

3

The 5 Big Rules

Most students come to school knowing about "home rules." The majority of them have a specific bedtime, for instance, rules about doing homework before watching television and rules of behavior in the house.

Use these "home rules" as a foundation for establishing classroom rules. The very first day of school spend time talking about "our classroom family." During the next two or three days, mention the need for rules in a family, especially one with many children and only one adult. Discuss the need to set up rules to make it fair for everyone in the room including the teacher.

For example, you might lead the students into a discussion of how it feels to be called "stupid." Ask students if they have ever been called names. Spend time talking as a group about the feelings you get when you are called bad, vulgar names. Do these words make you feel glad? Sad? Do you want to hit someone for calling you names?

ROLE PLAYING

It is important when discussing feelings to use more than words to illustrate what happens inside people when they are called bad names. Role playing not only allows students to hear but also to see these feelings on someone's face when others are rude.

Tell the students you are going to play some games which will help them understand how important it is to think of others' feelings.

Here is an example:

Boy 1 played by Randy

Boy 2 played by Ted

Teacher played by Mrs. Smith

Teacher takes the boys outside the room and tells them how she wants them to role-play their parts. Mrs. Smith, Randy and Ted return to the classroom.

Mrs. Smith: "Randy, you were telling me you took a trip to Yellowstone National Park this summer. What did you enjoy the most about the park?"

Before Randy can answer, Ted yells out from across the room: "That's a dumb place to go. I went there last year and it's . . ."

Mrs. Smith: "Randy, how did you feel not having time to answer the question I asked and how did it feel to have Ted say you went to a "dumb place?"

Randy: "I felt sad and hurt that Ted would yell out when I was trying to talk and then say Yellowstone was a dumb place to go. I loved it there. I wanted to tell the class about the mother bear and two baby cubs I saw but Ted wouldn't let me."

Mrs. Smith: "Class, do you see how Ted's yelling out and not giving Randy time to answer was wrong? It took away from Randy's ability to be allowed to give the answer he wanted to share. Class, how did Randy's face look when Ted yelled out at him?"

Spend several minutes letting students talk about this situation and how they might feel.

Mrs. Smith: "Ted, now I want you to look at Randy and say, 'I'm sorry, Randy.' "

Ted apologizes.

Mrs. Smith: "Class, do you think we need a rule about talking out so this won't happen again in our class?"

Have the class discuss the wording for a rule with help from you. When they agree on a specific rule about talking out in the classroom, have the students vote. Then write the rule on the chalkboard.

HIP TIP After the vote about talking out in class, take a moment to go over the right times to talk in class. Example: raise your hand, wait until the teacher recognizes you, then talk.

Now select two girls as role-players to illustrate how students should not behave in the classroom. Have Jennifer stick her foot out in the aisle and trip Amanda as she walks to the drinking fountain.

Mrs. Smith: "Amanda, how did you feel when Jennifer tripped you and made you fall against Brandon's desk?"

Amanda: "Awful! I felt silly and stupid and angry that Jennifer would do that to me."

Mrs. Smith: "Jennifer, why did you do that to Amanda?"

Jennifer: "'Cause she wouldn't let me play with her on recess."

Mrs. Smith: "Jennifer, that is not the way we treat classmates in this room. I want you to apologize to Amanda now."

Jennifer: "I'm sorry, Amanda."

Again lead the class into a discussion of why we need to have particular rules and how much more harmony we have in a classroom when we all obey the rules.

In the next few days, continue to role play and discuss the type of rules needed in the classroom.

SELECTING THE RULES

Depending upon the age and the needs of your students, the type of rules and their number will vary. Older students' rules will have a different wording from rules for first graders and they may also need a few more than primary students. Caution: Do not over-load your class with too many rules. Make a few and make them direct and to the point.

Here are five rules which one class finally settled upon. They are typical rules although your class may use different words.

1. LISTEN. In order to learn and get smarter, students must listen to their teacher, to other students and to the lessons as they are presented.

2. WORK WELL. This means that students should try to do their very best work at school. Working well means getting smarter and feeling good about oneself, and is reflected in good grades.

3. KNOW WHEN TO TALK. Students coming back to school after summer vacation are used to talking whenever they please. In order to learn, they need times when they do not talk. At other times it is important to talk and participate in class discussions. (This is when you need to decide if you want the students to raise their hands before talking).

4. KNOW WHEN TO USE YOUR HANDS AND FEET. Kicking, shoving and hitting are ongoing problems. Students need to understand that each of them can come to school without fear of being hurt. Discuss again the "our family" concept of treating each other with respect. This rule will remind students not to bother others. Then lead the class into a discussion about using hands and feet at the right times such as playing on the playground and using hands for writing, asking to talk and doing art work.

5. REPORTING. Countless valuable minutes are lost when students tattle. Talk about the precious time spent away from learning. Explain to the class about "Reporting" which means a student should come to the teacher only to say that a child has been hurt or is ill. All other problems must wait until the daily Class Meeting. (See Chapter 10).

Now, have your class talk over the rules presented and vote on them. The five with the most votes are written on the chalkboard. They remain there until Friday night when they are erased. Every Monday they are ceremoniously rewritten on the chalkboard. During the first month of school, go over the rules daily. Later, review them only on Monday.

HIP TIP It is vital that students have a say in the choice of rules or they will have little meaning for them. Based upon the role playing exercises, lead students to understand that rules help to protect our rights and make us more responsible for our actions. Also, that minding the rules helps a student build self-esteem and confidence in being a good citizen not only at school, but in the home and in the neighborhood.

RESPONSIBILITY FOR LEARNING

We need to help students understand they are responsible for their learning. One way of doing this is to point out that the best learning takes place when students are listening, following along in the textbook and actively taking part in class discussions.

In each class I've had in the past 20 years, at least three students (and sometimes more!) had no idea why they were in school and no intention of learning. Instead, they would sit, play and bother others. These students are likely to become dropouts later.

In order to help forestall this, we at the elementary level need to make these failure-prone students aware of their choice to fail while they are still in the lower grades.

GRAPHING

One visual way to help students grasp their responsibility in school is to draw graphs frequently on the overhead projector or chalkboard illustrating success and failure. During the first week of school it is important to draw a "Success/Failure" graph each day. Then throughout the year, as needed, draw a graph and discuss the choices students have to be smart students or failures. (See drawing on page 20.)

Use brightly colored overhead projector pens to do this. Draw a large rectangle on the overhead. During the first week of school, place the days (Monday, Tuesday, Wednesday, etc.) and underneath the dates: Sept. 4th, Sept. 5th, etc.

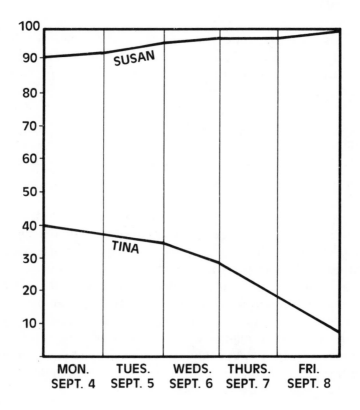

THE SUCCESS / FAILURE GRAPH

Then on the left side of the rectangle write the numbers 0, 10, 20, 30, . . . to 100 from bottom up to the top.

Tell the class about two students in another school. Call these students by any name except for the names in your classroom. Example: Susan and Tina.

Explain to the class that Susan pays attention in class, does her homework and is interested in getting smart this year. Say: "Look at the green line I'm drawing. Susan began school on Monday by doing her math and reading and she starts out making 90 percent on the first day. The next day she gave an oral book report and she is now up to 95 percent in her grades." Show that by Friday, Susan will be making 100 percent in school.

Now tell the class about Tina. Explain that Tina brings toys to school and hides them in her desk so she can play with them. She also spends her time looking around the room and not listening to the teacher. She forgets to take home her homework and she is often tardy and misses part of reading several days a week.

Draw a red line for Tina showing she only did half her math and got 40 percent the first day. She missed reading the second day and got zero and by the end of the week she was spending most of the day playing with things in her desk and ended up with a zero grade for the week in most subjects.

Explain to the class that what this means is that Tina does not care. She *chooses* not to be smart.

Then ask the students which line they would like to be — the green or the red. Ask, "Which line do you *choose?*" Explain again that the choice is up to them.

Each day vary the graph using different names and some days talking mostly about behavior choices. Illustrate on the graph what happens when poor behavior keeps students from learning and interferes with making good grades.

Follow each graphing lesson with a few minutes of open discussion.

MORNING GREETING

Another way to reinforce the idea that being smart is a choice is to use a daily greeting as a reminder to students that they come to school for a purpose: to learn.

This greeting ceremony or "catechism" might be like this:

Teacher: Good morning, boys and girls.

Students: Good morning, Mrs. Smith.

Teacher: Why did you come to school today?

Students: To get smarter.

Teacher: Why did Mrs. Smith come to school today?

Students: To help me get smarter.

Teacher: How many teachers do we have in our room today? (When parents are helping they should be included in the count).

Students: Two.

Teacher: How many students do we have in the room?

Students: Thirty-one.

Teacher: And that is why we have rules in our room. Tell me rule number one. (Teacher walks to the chalkboard and points to rule number one and the students read all the rules in unison).

Do the greeting in its entirety as needed to remind students about being smarter and the rules. At other times, only go over the initial greeting to where the students say, "To get smarter." You'll find this a great way to begin each day.

In this chapter we have talked about the importance of rules and of helping students to understand why they are in school. In the next chapter you will see how "making points" can be a positive and enthusiastic experience for students in your successful classroom.

CHAPTER 4

POINTS PAY OFF

4

Points Pay Off

Children have a natural interest in competing whether on the playground, in a spelling bee or seeing who can get to their seats first. This competitive spirit makes the HIP system function well day after day and month after month in the classroom.

The method centers around the three stations in the room. Here is an example of how to begin the first day of school: As the students file into the room, ask them to remain at the back. Explain that you are not going to assign seats to them. This will come as a happy surprise to most of them. Invite them to look over the room and decide where they would like to sit. Assure them that they can choose a seat by a friend, but they must remember that if they talk or do not pay attention that you must move them. Point out that as long as they behave they can sit in the seat they have selected.

Ask them to walk quietly to the seat they would like. Later in the day, post their names on their desks. I find it best to write their names on sentence strips, then cover the strips with an overhanging piece of Contact paper. Place the name on the front of each student's desk where it will remain until the last day of school. The students may then remove the name tag and take it home with them as a souvenir of the year.

The students remain at their chosen desks all year except for the president and vice president. (See chapter 10). However, after the first week if certain seating combinations selected by students do not work out, I do move them. I also monitor stations all year to be sure none is ever overloaded with discipline problems. These problem students are divided among the three stations.

Always keep one unused desk available in one station with needed supplies ready for a new student. This empty desk often serves as a barrier between two students who need to have space between them. When a new student arrives, the desk is ready for him or her. Immediately obtain another empty desk to repeat the process, usually placing it in another station.

There may not be an equal number of students in the stations but this does not present any problems.

NAMING THE STATIONS

The day school begins, discuss with the class about the manner in which the desks are arranged. Bring up the word "station," and ask a student to look up the definition in the dictionary and read it to the class. Follow this by explaining to the students that each station will need a name. This can be done during the first week by ballot within each station, by suggestions from the teacher, or by a voice vote from each station. Again the students should take part, under the guidance of the teacher, in this process.

Here is how one classroom chose to select their names.

In a discussion led by the teacher, the students began to talk about the position of their stations in the classroom. It soon became apparent that the three stations were arranged on the north side of the room, the south and the west. One student even brought in a compass to verify the location and the students unanimously decided to call themselves "North," "South," and "West" stations.

The station names should be easy to say and only a word or two in length because they will be used constantly during the year. Here are a few more ideas: Use a patriotic theme such as "Red,

White and Blue." Or, perhaps, "Wagon Train," or names of trees, birds or perhaps the names of football teams.

After the selection, the names are printed in the most prominent place on the chalkboard. (See drawing on page 28.) Explain to the class that each station can earn points by behaving, following directions and participating in classroom activities. Also, stress that messing around, not following directions and disrupting the class can result in a loss of points for a station. Tell the students the points will remain on the chalkboard all week in full view of any visitors coming into the room.

It is vital to begin the point system as soon as the station names are listed on the chalkboard. Example: After the recess you might say, "I like the quiet way each station walked into the classroom after recess this morning. Each station earned five points."

Immediately encourage the class to applaud their good work in earning their first points. I use clapping a great deal during the day to reinforce the positive feelings that come from earning points.

Here is how we do our "three clap:"
Teacher counts: "One, two, three"
Class: One giant clap
Teacher counts: "One, two, three"
Class: One giant clap
Teacher counts: "One, two, three"
Class: One final giant clap

By counting, and doing one single clap together, you cut out students who clap on and on trying to be silly. This also takes care of the student who always wants to be the last one to make a noise when clapping. This method works well and gives students the thrill of competing to see if they can all end at the same instant. Another variation, especially for older students, would be to substitute snapping their fingers for clapping.

DISPLAYING POINTS

A new point count is begun on the chalkboard each Monday and continues through Friday dismissal.

HONOR POINT CHART

HIP TIP Use the adding and subtracting of points as a way of teaching math facts. Students enjoy orally helping the teacher add points to their stations. They also get a thrill assisting the teacher as she subtracts points from a rival station. When an adding or subtracting mistake is made, at least one station will let you know of the error in a most resounding manner!

WAYS TO EARN POINTS

When any adult walks into the room, be it parent, the nurse, or the custodian, and says to me, "My, but you have a fine class," each station automatically earns five points. When the principal says "great class" the stations earn 10 points. The points are added just as soon as the guest leaves the room. I explain to the class what the guest said and how proud I was of them. After I add the points to the totals, we all clap.

Stations can also earn points by being the first cleaned up and sitting quietly when it is time to go out to recess or P.E. — also when they come in quietly.

When students leave the classroom and your control, you can emphasize good behavior by telling them they can still earn points. Take, for example, a trip to the library for their weekly lesson given by the school librarian. You can tell them as they walk out the door, that when you pick them up 45 minutes later you will add 25 points to each station's total if no names appear on the library chalkboard from their station. However, if you note, for example, Jason's name on the chalkboard from North Station, then that station will not earn their 25 points.

This works very well when taking a class to an assembly. Remind them you have a notebook and will note names of misbehaving students. This helps to keep problem students in line. I've had teachers say to me after an assembly program, "Your students were so well behaved in the assembly this morning." As soon as we return to the classroom, I pass this information on to the class; we clap and add points to each station's total.

The HIP program is not designed to be a "teacher controlled discipline plan." Instead, the system functions whether the teacher is in the room or not since the peer pressure continues to operate.

This is also true when substitutes arrive. In my top desk drawer is a bright red folder with "HIP TIPS for subs" spelled out. The students are well aware that when I'm away from the classroom, that they are still able to earn extra points by continuing to behave.

Tell the class that if you return and find the substitute has had a good day in the class, then each station will receive, for example 25 or 30 points. But, should one student from a station misbehave so much that the name is noted on the sub's report, that station earns no points.

Students also become creative in thinking of other ways to earn points. One boy returned from recess with a $5.00 bill he had found. After sending the money to the office, I had the boy stand with me in the front of the room while we did our "three clap" and then his station received 20 points for having such an honest student.

Another boy, I've noted, frequently stays after school when his station needs points. Without my saying a word, he gets on his hands and knees and crawls under all the desks and picks up pieces of paper, lost pencils and erasers. When he finishes, he casually walks up to me and says, "Mrs. W., look at the clean room. Tomorrow morning, after flag salute, could I remind you of what I did so my station can get 10 extra points?"

HIP TIP When students are more restless, such as before and after a holiday like Halloween and before vacations or on windy days, be very generous with points.

FOUR ADDITIONAL WAYS TO EARN POINTS

The point system is a fantastic way to get things from home. Here are some examples:

• Five points for each station member who brought in a milk carton when we made ice cream in our room.

• Five points to each station for students who brought in an embroidery hoop we needed for an art project

• Five points for each person in a station who brought back their signed report card

• Ten points to a station for any student whose parents attended one of our special class programs

You can be very creative in ways students may earn points. It is indeed rewarding to see how hard they will work in order to earn points for their stations.

Points should be awarded the first thing in the morning for those bringing things. Students are quick to remind you to get to the board and get the points recorded. Again, only the teacher can add or take away points from the total.

Following opening morning activities, move to the chalkboard to see which station is ahead. Example: West Station. Ask those students in West Station who brought back their report cards to raise their hands. Collect the cards and count them and multiply the number by five and add this to the total score for West Station, then call upon the other stations. Totalling points in the morning should not take more than three or four minutes at most.

POINT REMOVAL

Points can also be subtracted from a station's score. Example: If during a math lesson, I look up from the overhead projector and see a girl in South Station talking to her neighbor I say, "Someone in South Station is visiting and not listening so I must take a point away from South Station."

If that same girl continues to bother those around her I will use her name saying, "Michele is continuing to bother those around her and not paying attention so she is choosing to lose a point for

South Station."

We do want students at that station to let Michele know that she let them down.

They may turn around and say quietly, "Oh, Michele." But they cannot yell out, "OH, MICHELE," for then I take off another point.

Points can also be removed when a station runs into the room and makes noise. Immediately say, "North Station was being extra loud today, they chose to lose five points." Stations can lose points when a student fools around and holds up the class from getting started, for example, on math. Points are also deducted when a student throws a pencil or eraser across the room or gets angry and swears at a classmate.

POINT REWARDS

Students quickly learn that the station with the most points gets a big payoff. Here are some examples:

• Any food, such as cupcakes, brought for celebrating birthdays goes first to the station with the most points

• The station with the most points goes out first for recess and lunch

• During an art project, the station with the most points is first to select their paper and drawing materials

• On field trips the station with the most points gets the choice of seats on the school bus

• And finally, and most important of all, the station with the most points on Friday afternoon at dismissal time gets to pick ALL THE JOBS IN THE CLASSROOM for the following week.

HIP TIP Before you leave on Friday afternoon, be sure to record the station with the most points in your Lesson Plan book so you won't forget.

In the next chapter, you will discover why choosing classroom jobs is the BIG PRIZE at the Monday morning Job Meeting.

CHAPTER 5

MONDAY MATTERS

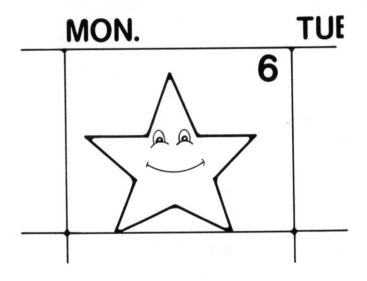

5

Monday Matters

*B*oys and girls look forward to Halloween, Valentine's Day and the day before summer vacation. HIP students look forward to Mondays as well.

The heart of the HIP system is the Monday morning Job Meeting at which the station with the most points for the previous week chooses the job assignments for this week. (Each station begins anew each Monday and works hard to try to be the winners for that week.)

The first day of school began by talking to the class about Honor Incentive Points and how points can be earned by obeying the rules. During the second week the rules were voted on. By the third Monday in September, you should introduce the Job Meeting to the students.

Some intermediate teachers may feel their students will not buy into jobs as a payoff for earning points. Chapter 13 provides some ideas which should work well in these classrooms. On the other hand, you may wish to adapt ideas in this chapter to your own particular classroom.

HIP TIP As soon as you walk into the classroom on Monday mornings go to the chalkboard, write "Honor Points" and underneath list the names of the stations. Then check your Lesson Plan book for the winning station from Friday. Say that North Station won. Then go to the chalkboard and draw a star next to North Station. The star drawing will save you many, many minutes during the opening morning activities telling all the students which station won.

Before I show you how to conduct the Job Meeting, here are some examples of typical jobs in a classroom. Again, remember how important it is to have input from students. You may be surprised at what they feel needs to be done in your classroom. Having had a voice, they will energetically take part in keeping the room in good order.

DEFINITIONS OF JOBS

Bailiff: The bailiff serves in place of the teacher when the teacher is talking to parents in the room, for example, or carrying on a Class Meeting. (See chapter 10.)

If a problem develops while the teacher is busy the teacher will say, "Bailiff, someone in South Station just threw an eraser. Go to the board and take off five points."

While the teacher conducts the Class Meeting the bailiff will sit in a chair underneath the Honor Points and add or subtract points at the teacher's direction. (See drawing on page 37.) *Only the teacher ever changes the totals.*

Paper person: This popular job involves passing out all paper to each station during the week. The student may distribute the paper individually to each student or select a person at each station to hand out papers. This position gives the student power in choosing special people to be the passers and is eagerly sought after.

**CHANGING POINTS ON THE
HONOR POINT CHART**

Light monitor: This job also gives the student a feeling of importance. The light monitor turns the light off for films, for the overhead projector, as needed, and turns lights off and on when coming and going for recess and lunch break.

Drape monitor: This student opens and closes the drapes for movies and for the overhead projector, as needed.

Ball monitor: This job is considered a most important position by students. The ball monitor is responsible for taking out physical education equipment as designated by the teacher for recess, lunch and during the P.E. period. The monitor picks a boy and girl each time to be in charge of the equipment on recess and lunch period.

The following jobs are done at specified times of the day, but without specific instruction from the teacher. The only need for change would be if the student assigned to the task is absent and the teacher selects the President, Vice President or a volunteer to fill in.

Flag monitor: The flag monitor walks forward each morning, gives the "Stand, salute, and pledge," directions and remains standing in the front until the class finishes the pledge and singing "America."

Book monitor: The book monitor makes sure the class library is neat and tidy.

Sink person: The student is in charge of keeping the sink and drainboard clean.

Closet person: The chosen student makes sure the closet area is kept neat at all times during the day.

Sweeper person: Five minutes before going home the sweeper person cleans the rug in the classroom. The student particularly enjoys being able to say to messy students, "Get that stuff cleaned up under your desk so I can sweep."

HIP TIP Give yourself a present if you do not have a rug in your classroom. Get one! After 20 years of teaching in rooms with vinyl tile floors and listening to students scaping noisy metal chairs and desks across the floor day after day, I decided I deserved a rug. I purchased two 22-foot strips of inexpensive indoor carpeting at a discount store. Then I got two fathers to come to the classroom and help me put down the carpeting which almost covered my entire room. We used carpet tape underneath to secure the rug to the floor. I then used Duct tape around the edges to stick the carpeting down. Hint — Be sure and check with your principal first to be sure you can do this. Your district may have rules about having all carpets sprayed with fire retardant first.

The morning after we put the carpet down, three mothers walked in to help me. They stopped, listened and smiled. One said to me, "Oh, it is so quiet in here. What a difference it makes in the noise level." I wish I'd put down carpeting 20 years ago!

Of course, your classroom may need different job classifications. It's important to have a job for each student in a station. Only students in the winning station are ever eligible for jobs, otherwise, you defeat the purpose of the HIP system.

JOB MEETING

This is how you begin: If North Station won, begin by congratulating the station for doing a fantastic job, then lead a three clap to let North Station know you, along with their classmates, recognize they are winners!

Students in a station can nominate each other if they wish. Many students, however, want a particular job and the meeting goes more smoothly when they are allowed to nominate themselves for a position.

Teacher: "Is there anyone in North Station who would like to nominate themselves or someone else to be the Bailiff for this week?"

Janice (standing): "Mrs. Smith, I would like to nominate myself this week to be Bailiff."

Teacher: "Thank you, Janice. I'm recording your nomination."

Then perhaps one or two other students will make nominations. Record each of these names.

Teacher: "Now does anyone else in North Station have a nomination for bailiff? If not, we will now vote. Will the following students put their heads on their desks and close their eyes: Janice, Tom and Brad. Now would everyone else in the class please stand."

HIP TIP By having the students stand for the voting and then sit down after casting their vote, you can be almost sure no student voted twice.

Teacher: "Remember students, you may vote for yourself. Now, will all those students who wish to have Janice as your bailiff please raise your hands?"

The teacher counts and records this information then the students who voted for Janice sit down. Continue in this manner until all those nominated have had their votes recorded. Even if no student is still standing, call out the remaining names so no one feels left out.

Teacher: Congratulates the student elected, invites student applause then walks over to the chalkboard and writes the title "Jobs" at the top and "Save" after the title so no one will erase this until Friday dismissal.

Underneath the title she writes "Bailiff" — "Janice." See drawing on page 41.)

The meeting continues until all jobs have been taken — normally about 30 minutes. Keep in mind that some students may not want a job or if the job they want is taken by someone else they may choose to sit out the remainder of the meeting without trying for another position.

In this chapter you've learned how to conduct the Job Meeting. In our next chapter you'll discover what an important part the physical education program plays in the HIP system classroom.

JOB CHART IN HIP CLASSROOM

CHAPTER 6

KICKING TOWARD SUCCESS

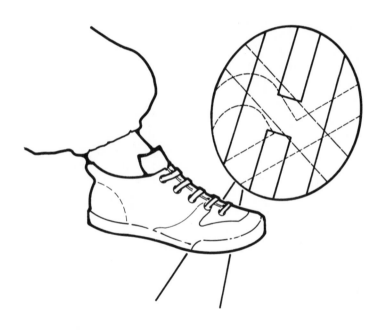

6

Kicking Toward Success

*W*hether they are six or sixteen, if you ask students their favorite subject, most will overwhelmingly say, "P.E."

Teachers who tap into their students' enthusiasm and energy for physical education activities can create an even more successful classroom.

In the HIP system, physical education plays a vital part in the daily program. Again, depending upon your class and your school's daily schedule, you can adjust the P.E. program to fit your students' needs.

The HIP method uses the P.E. program to help students learn to cooperate with one another, with the teacher, and with the umpire, or whoever is making the decisions on plays.

Before school opens in September, have the year's plan in mind for your physical education program so you can direct your class in working out a cooperative schedule for the months ahead. If you don't plan, the students' eagerness for a specific game might lock you into one activity for the school year. This is certainly not wrong but if you want to encourage your class to explore a variety of activities, make this clear at the beginning.

Example: You may wish to have your class spend the first ten minutes of each physical education period doing exercises. Then you may want to encourage your students to play soccer one week and kickball the next.

SELECTING TEAM CAPTAINS

Here is how to begin the P.E. program with your class: After the Monday Job Meeting, and prior to your scheduled P.E. period, arrange a few minutes to select captains and team members.

Since North Station had the most points as we observed in the last chapter, they will pick the captains for the week.

Frequently everyone in a station wants to be captain and anyone in a winning station may be nominated to be captain, even someone already elected to another job. Follow the same procedure for nominations for captain as you do for Job Meeting.

After a student is nominated to be a captain, ask the student whom he or she would like to have as co-captain. The student can select ANYONE IN THE CLASSROOM to be co-captain and usually there will be plenty of eager classmates to choose from.

Record all the nominations and conduct the election just as you did for the jobs, having students stand and going through the entire list. The two students with the most votes become captains for the week. Have them select their teams in any manner you feel would be best, perhaps varying the process from week to week. Also, captains should alternate sexes as they pick their teams.

After the teams are selected, they huddle with their captain to decide upon a team name. At the first of the year, you might want to help the class pick out team names. Example: Suggest the first week that they choose a two word title with the first being a color and the second an animal. Students become creative in coming up with names such as Pink Alligators, Purple Elephants and Silver Unicorns. The second week suggest they pick names from the science lesson. Example: This week the class will be studying beetles. They will come up with interesting names such as Creepy Beetles or Monster Beetles or Demon Beetles.

Put both team names on the board and record the ongoing

total of runs or points for each day's activity.

The captains serve for one week. New captains, teams and names are chosen the following Monday. This gives more students the opportunity to serve as captains and to develop leadership qualities in the classroom.

HIP TIP Some captains will be more popular than others and tend to be chosen over and over. If this happens and you get grumbling from other students, consider holding a Class Meeting to discuss the problem (See Chapter 10). I did this and the class voted that Angie, who had been captain four weeks out of six, should not be a captain again for one month. Angie also agreed that this was fair.

Games such as kickball or baseball start Monday and end on Friday. Keep track of which team is up first and which student leads off each day. At the end of a game, indicate on your sheet the student who will go up first the following day. That way everyone gets a turn in order and no one is left out.

HIP TIP Some students, particularly girls, are timid or awkward in athletics. Encourage the more talented players in your class to work with reluctant classmates on particular skills during their recess and lunch breaks. Peer tutoring can achieve fantastic results with shy students, resulting in the build up of self-esteem and physical competence in both the student and peer teacher.

WALKING THE PERIMETER

This is a device which uses the physical education period as a time for you to discipline misbehaving students who will not respond to classroom peer pressure.

Example: Russ has been bugging people all week. He has repeatedly lost points for his station. Russ has a favorite subject:

physical education. He loves to play soccer. On a particularly bad day, warn Russ by putting his name on the chalkboard. Tell him that if he breaks another rule he CHOOSES to put himself on the Perimeter during P.E. today.

"Perimeter" is a line of your choosing on the blacktop or an imaginary line between two trees or any two points you designate as the "Perimeter line" for your students. If you have a blacktop, pick a long painted line which parallels the area where you will be playing, for example, either kickball or soccer. Since Russ loves to play soccer, you'll make much more impact if you play soccer on the day Russ walks the Perimeter. No matter where you are playing, you must be able to see Russ walking the line from where you'll be standing during P.E.

If Russ breaks another classroom rule, tell him that you are writing the word "Perimeter" after his name and he must walk the Perimeter today while his classmates play soccer.

Prior to students walking the Perimeter, remind them that they must not run, play, fool around or stop to rest while walking the Perimeter. Let them know that if they do, they are CHOOSING to walk the Perimeter the next day and the next, if necessary. Emphasize that this is the student's responsibility, you will not issue any reminders.

While out on P.E. be aware of Russ and what he is doing but do not say a word to him. Rather, wait until you return to the classroom. If he behaved, ask him to come up and erase his own name off the board. Then have the class do a three clap. If he did not behave, say, "Russ I saw you playing with a tennis ball while you were walking the Perimeter today. You CHOSE to walk the Perimeter again tomorrow."

You should not have many students walking the Perimeter as most of them will obey class rules in order to participate in P.E.

In this chapter you have learned about the importance of the physical education program to teach student cooperation both in and out of the class.

In the next chapter you'll learn about the most sought-after position in the HIP system: Class President.

CHAPTER 7

CLASS PRESIDENT

7

Class President

*F*ootball fans sitting in the stands hold up giant gloves with an enlarged index finger proclaiming their team is number one. Auto manufacturers tout their car as the number one automobile sold in the country. Car rental agencies compete yearly for the title, "We're Number One." Being number one brings status, clout and name recognition to the winner.

Each month in the HIP classroom, one student is elected president and another vice president, the number one and two status positions. Students eagerly look forward to entering the competition to be class leaders.

Prior to the first election, it is important to spend time talking to the students about elections and how they are run in our country. Discuss the Democratic and Republican parties and how several candidates run for the Office of President every four years although only one is elected.

Spend time discussing how a person gets others to vote for him or her. Your students need to see the value in being friendly, kind and outgoing so classmates will know them. As the teacher, you are already aware that certain students stand out. These exceptional boys and girls exhibit leadership qualities and the ability to talk in front of a group. Usually they are popular among their classmates. But all students need to know that anyone can run for class president and anyone can win.

HIP TIP At the beginning of the school year talk about the shy, quiet student who seldom speaks out as opposed to the disruptive or problem maker student. Encourage your quiet students by saying, "I know you're just as talented as the others in the room but we don't know you. I want you to begin to make friends, be friendly and 'let your light shine.' "

Also address the problem student who, due to poor behavior, is unpopular in the classroom. These students need to understand that their behavior keeps them from being the type of person others want in leadership positions. Encourage problem students to become the type of friend others respect, admire and choose to nominate for president.

PREPARING FOR THE PRESIDENTIAL ELECTION

Here are some important facts your students need to know before you conduct the first presidential election:
- The election will always be held the first Monday of the month just prior to the Job Meeting.
- The winning station nominates candidates or members of the winning station can nominate themselves.
- When nominated, a candidate must then pick a running mate who can be FROM ANY STATION IN THE CLASSROOM.
- After votes are counted, the president will be the student with the most votes and the vice president will be the student with second most votes. In other words, all names for president and vice president are put on a long list. Then the vote is taken. The student receiving the most votes becomes president. The student receiving the next largest number of votes becomes vice president.

THE PRESIDENTIAL ELECTION

On the first Monday of the month, before the Job Meeting, hold the presidential election. Follow the instructions given above. But, if for example, several students get six votes each and the others get only one or two then do a run off for those with six votes each. In the final count, as mentioned, the student with the most votes becomes president and the next vote getter is named the vice president.

This election is conducted in a slightly different way from the Job Meeting to give the presidential election more honor, more ceremony befitting a presidential candidate. Hint: After you and your students have gone through a couple of these elections the entire selection process should not take more than ten minutes.

PRESIDENTIAL MOVES

Following the election, the president and vice president will move from their current stations. The president will sit near the main door in the room and the vice president near the other door if there is one. (See drawing page 54.)

One responsibility of the president, as leader of the class, is to walk the students outside to a prearranged meeting place during all fire drills. But in case there should ever be a fire and the main door is blocked, the vice president takes the class out the other door.

After sharing this information with your students, you're ready for the next step.

PRESIDENTIAL RESPONSIBILITIES

At the first presidential election, explain to the class what the president's and vice president's duties include. Here are some from a typical classroom:

• The president and vice president, no matter which station they are now in, will move after the election as we have noted. The

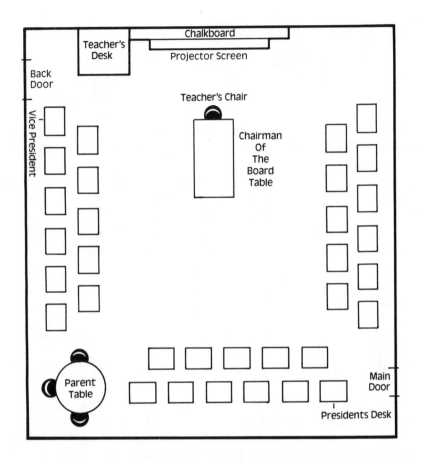

**SEATING PLAN FOR PRESIDENT
AND VICE PRESIDENT**

president answers all knocks at the main door and escorts guests into the classroom.

- The president conducts Telling The News, and Tell Time in the primary grades and Sharing at the intermediate level.
- As mentioned, the president leads the class outside for all fire drills.
- The president is the line leader for the entire month. As leader, the president is always first in line going out and coming in.
- The president takes messages to the office for the teacher.
- The president serves as a substitute for any absent student who holds a job such as the flag monitor or the sweeper.

Here are the responsibilities for the vice president:

- During a fire drill, if the main door is blocked, the vice president leads the class outside to the designated place for fire drills.
- At all other times, the vice president is the last person leaving the classroom, making sure everyone is out of the room so the teacher can lock the door.
- The vice president is the last one in line when returning to the classroom from recess and lunch and seeks to get all stragglers into line when the bell rings.
- The vice president takes over when the president is absent.

HIP TIP Use the movement of president and vice president at the first of the month as a natural time, if needed, to move a student or two out of a station and into another. Example: When the president moves near the door, move out a student who is misbehaving or getting too friendly with those around him or her. This can be done without seeming to point out any one student as being a problem.

In this chapter you have learned how to hold a presidential election and the importance and prestige of the positions held by the president and vice president in the classroom.

In the next chapter you're going to find out the two most important functions the president fills in the successful classroom.

CHAPTER 8

STATION BREAKS

8

Station Breaks

*T*he majority of children love to talk. They talk to themselves, they talk to their pets, they talk to each other.

The HIP system uses this natural ability by providing times each day for oral expression in the classroom. These vocal activities, led by the president, provide a time for students to develop leadership skills, speaking competency and help in overcoming fears when speaking before a group.

HIP teachers are constantly seeking ways to demonstrate democracy in action. Through the use of Telling The News and Tell Time, and in the intermediate grades, Sharing, each student's presentation is important; whether a current event, something heard on television, or showing off a new family pet.

Here are explanations for the oral activities found in HIP classrooms:

TELLING THE NEWS

In many classrooms, children in Kindergarten and First grade, bring a special toy to school, tell where they got the toy, how much it costs (if known) and where they keep it in their house. The term most commonly used for this activity is "Show and Tell."

In HIP rooms the term is "Telling the News." This expression encompasses the Show and Tell idea but it goes beyond it for students in HIP rooms are urged to look at newspapers, books and magazines.

Those who take the time to read an interesting article in the paper, for example, and present it to the class, earn extra points for their station. This generates interest in sharing current events with the class and is more educational than showing off a new toy.

TELL TIME

Tell Time is simply telling about a subject which interests the child or would teach the other students something of interest. Example: A student might tell about visiting a grandfather who lives in the California mountains. He or she might tell about hunting for gold with the grandfather. The student would describe how cold the water was in the stream, how to hold the gold pan and tell about any nuggets found.

One student might choose to talk about going to a science museum, while someone else would talk about "how scared I was when my little sister swallowed some aspirin and we had to rush her to the hospital in the middle of the night."

Tell Time serves as a vehicle whereby students can vent their feelings. Example: Robert requested the teacher ring the bell for Tell Time. Since the class was behind in completing a math assignment, the teacher hesitated. After two more urgent requests from Robert the teacher rang the bell. Soon it became apparent why Robert needed Tell Time just then. His father, in the Air Force, had been transferred to Japan. Robert explained where his father would be stationed (a student held the world globe) and he told how much he was missing his father and how long it was until the rest of the family could go to Japan.

PREPARING STUDENTS FOR TELLING THE NEWS AND TELL TIME

In the HIP classroom in September, it is important to prepare students for Telling The News and Tell Time. Some students shy away from getting up in front of classmates. This is even more true for students who are new in the room. These fears need to be recognized.

HIP TIP As students sit in their seats, the first week of the new school year, lead the class in an oral discussion by throwing out questions such as: "Where did you go this summer?" or, "What is your favorite food?" or "Tell me about your pet." As you go from student to student, assure them that they can say "pass" and the next time they can share with the group.

The second week begin to call upon those who wish to talk. Say, "You may stand at your seat and talk or you may come up and stand by the Chairman of the Board table." To build excitement say, "Now Randy in South Station will bring us a special report." Or, "Carmen has a newsflash for all of us from North Station." Use terms like, "special bulletin, in-depth report, and flash." Since students watch so much television, they will relate to these terms at once.

During the first month of school, you are the model for conducting Telling The News and Tell Time. How you conduct the meeting is the way the future president will direct the meetings from October onward.

THE PRESIDENT PRESIDES

After the presidential election in early October, the president will take over conducting Telling The News and Tell Time while sitting in the teacher's chair at the Chairman of the Board table. The bailiff sits in a chair near the HIP chart. During Telling The

News and Tell Time, the bailiff, under directions from the teacher, removes or adds points to specific stations if necessary.

The president begins with the station with the most points. Example: South Station is in the lead. The president would ask all students in South Station who brought something to share to raise their hands. The president selects a student to come to the front of the room.

After the student makes the presentation, the president should be prepared to lead a discussion. Here are sample questions: "Who gave you the old coin?" "How much is it worth?" Or, "Could any of you bring a coin book so we could look it up?" Then the president opens the discussion to the class members. Frequently, the answers to students' questions will clarify a quickly stated presentation given by a nervous, shy student.

After all students in South Station who wish to share have had a turn, the president turns to the station with the next most points and then to the last station, giving all who want an opportunity to share. Some days half the class might share while on other days maybe only five or six might come prepared. The entire activity should not take over 15 minutes. If the meeting tends to lag, urge students to shorten their presentations to a few sentences.

During Telling The News, you should be able to walk quietly back to the parent table where you can relax while the class president conducts the meeting — but this is not always possible. Sometimes, depending upon the makeup of your class, you may need to sit in the vacant president's chair in the station. In this way you take an active part in Telling The News if you find students fail to cooperate with the class president. Classes can be very different and you must decide what works best for you with each one.

PARADE

At the end of Telling The News, the president announces, "Parade." The president stands near the Chairman of the Board table and waits for all students who participated in Telling The News to line up behind him or her. At the direction of the teacher, the president can lead the parade, or ask the bailiff to lead.

The parade is simply a HIP classroom activity which gives students an opportunity to show at close range what they brought to school. They can also answer individual questions from students as they pass in front of their desks. HIP students may choose to stay at their desks but they are urged to move to the front of the "U" and stand quietly while the parade passes in front of them. Only students who brought items for Telling The News will be in the parade. Afterwards all large items should be placed on the window counter, or some designated area and small items inside students' desks.

ADDITIONAL PARADE IDEAS

The parade need not be limited to a daily Telling The News. When a parent comes to school to show off a student's turtle, for instance, ask the president to stand at the front of the room and lead a special parade which might only include the student, the turtle and the president as leader.

When other classes offer to come to your room to exhibit their art work, for example, ask the bailiff or president to lead the parade of the visiting students.

The teacher signals when the parade is over by ringing a bell, making a prearranged arm motion, or sounding a note on the piano. Students should return immediately to their desks or lose points.

Students need to be aware, however, that if they play with toys brought for Telling The News during the day they are choosing to have points removed from their station.

HIP TIP Make a firm rule at the beginning of the year that all Telling The News items must go home at the end of each day. The first few weeks make such an announcement just prior to dismissal, to help remind the class, but don't continue these daily reminders. Make it the students' responsibility. If students continually forget to take Telling The News items home, take points off that station.

SHARING

In the intermediate grades, Sharing is used as a way for older students to share a favorite hobby with fellow students, show off a skirt made during vacation or present a current event to the class.

In the HIP intermediate classroom, Sharing means students talk about, for example, a recent trip to the ocean, a personal happening, or add some additional information to a previous science lesson on rocks. The student may have taken the time to look up the definitions for obsidian, granite and limestone, or brought specimens from a rock collection.

When students do this extra work, their station should be awarded extra points, with the exact number reflecting the amount of work involved in researching and bringing the report to the class.

Sharing can also be a time for venting feelings for the student. Example: talking about the death of a grandparent, an upcoming move or being elected leader of a Cub Scout den.

HIP TIP At the beginning of the year, lay the ground rules for newspaper, television and magazine reports. Let students know you will not accept any reports on grisly murders, auto crashes or bombings. Students tend to get emotionally caught up in the gory details and pictures of such stories and miss the facts and students the following day may bring in an even more horrible story for an "I-can-top-that."

Whether teaching in the primary or intermediate grades, encourage students to bring in news which would serve as a learning experience for the entire class. Also, when a student talks on a subject where "big" words are used suggest that, if a student brings back a definition of the word the next day, a certain number of points can be earned for the station. Use this technique of reporting as a tool for expanding the class's knowledge on a variety of subjects.

In this chapter you've learned how Telling The News, Tell Time and Sharing are special ways you can use a student's zeal for talking as a learning experience for all students in the classroom.

You've also seen that Telling The News, Tell Time and Sharing are ways of building self-confidence, self-esteem and good oral expression skills in students.

In the next chapter you will discover how Telling The News, Tell Time and Sharing give you a welcome rest from your non-stop day.

CHAPTER 9

TIME OUT

9

Time Out

*S*urveys taken in classrooms indicate teachers make 500 decisions each hour, second only in number to air traffic controllers. No wonder harried, hassled and hurried teachers look forward to weekends so they can enroll in stress-reducing workshops.

But you need not wait until the weekend for a change of pace. In the HIP classroom, all you need to do is prearrange your schedule for a brief oasis of restful calm in your busy, busy day.

The HIP room is set up in such a manner that the Class President, after watching your example at the beginning of the school year, is well prepared to take over Telling The News, Tell Time or Sharing.

While the president does this, the bailiff sits at the Honor Point chart and adds or removes points. This makes HIP students aware that even when you are not in front of the room, the built-in disciplinary plan continues. The structure of the system provides you with your own personal "Time Out."

SCHEDULED SERENITY

Since you've scheduled for Telling The News, this is a perfect time to let the president take over for you.

On the other hand, Tell Time should be saved for the inevitable interruptions which arrive. Example: the principal needs to talk to you for a few minutes. Ring the bell, ask the students to clear their desks, then say, "President, please conduct Tell Time." This will give you time to devote all your attention to the principal, a parent or other unexpected visitors.

CONSECUTIVE NUMBERS

Students in the primary grades frequently have a problem saying and writing numbers, for example, from one to 100. Many can write a few in correct sequence but often they get mixed up when they get to numbers like 39. They cannot recall what comes next. The problem continues. They continually come to the teacher and ask, "What comes after 59, or 69 or 79?" One method for teaching individual students to count in order is to put them at a large table and give them one hundred pennies and a pencil and slips of paper and have them label each of the pennies in order from one to a hundred. This routine is very good when working with one student but is too difficult to arrange for a number of pupils needing extra help.

In the HIP classroom, students in the primary segment practice their numbers by writing from one onward as far as they can go, sometimes up into the thousands. Here is how to arrange this activity:

At the beginning of the year, plan an art activity where each pupil makes a number book. Provide each student with a manila folder. Using colored chalk on the chalkboard, design a Number Book for them as a model. The title can be "My Number Book" or "My Number Folder."

Hold a class discussion about the various ways students can decorate them. By suggesting a prize, or extra HIP points, for the top three winners, you can usually insure some spectacular art-work.

After the covers are finished, pass out five sheets of regular newsprint lined paper. Have the students fold the paper lengthwise in half and then again making four columns. Ask them to put their name on each sheet and number the pages in order. Staple the pages to the inside of the folder.

Instruct the students to begin writing number "1" and then "2" and on down the column. I use the overhead the first couple of days and write along with the class so I know they are following directions and doing the numbers correctly.

The object is to see how far students can write their numbers in correct order. Suggest when they are not sure of the next number, they can refer to an old, large telephone book which you can provide in the classroom.

Students love the competition and you'll hear them say to a neighbor, "I'm up to 1,800 now and I'm going to get to 2,000 by next week so I can go for the prize."

To continue this interest, you can have a drawing every Monday. Example: all students who reach 2,000 that day can enter. The three highest numbers drawn will be the students getting the prizes that Monday.

Soon after beginning this project, check to find at least one outstanding "consecutive number" student in each station to act as a helper. When visitors step into the room to talk to you, you can ask the class to take out their consecutive number books. Then ask the helpers in each station to walk around and assist those having problems. This is another way of providing you with a "Time Out" break, when needed.

Another idea which students, particularly in the intermediate grades, enjoy on a daily basis is a journal. Students can bring inex-pensive notebooks from home or they can cut good lined paper in half and cover front and back with construction paper to form the booklet. Again, have your students spend an art period designing a cover for the journal. Use competition, an art grade or HIP points as an incentive to do good work.

Each day have your students write a page about something

going on in the room, a new pet at home or something special going on in their lives. This gives students practice in creative writing and, since the teacher will not be grading this activity, it becomes even more enjoyable. Again, when the teacher needs a "Time Out" students can take out their journals. Some students may wish to share "special pages" during Sharing time. They should be encouraged to do this.

TIPS FOR TIME OUT

Now that you have several opportunities each day to take a change of pace, here are some do's and don'ts:

DON'T
• Reach for a stack of uncorrected papers while the Class President is conducting Telling The News or Tell Time. Let them wait. Give yourself the luxury of doing absolutely nothing during these few precious minutes. You owe it to yourself and to your students to relax.

• Rush to your desk and grab your class register and feverishly complete the monthly tabulation due in the office later in the day. Rather enjoy "the quiet now" and plan to do the detailed register when all the students are gone for the day.

• Dash up to the Chairman of the Board table and reach for your Lesson Plan book in hopes of getting a head start on writing lesson plans for the following week. Again, relax, enjoy! Even if you cannot be "Queen or King for a whole day," you can be for ten whole minutes!

DO
• Arrange a special place in the back of the room where you can rest during these time outs. Settle in the most comfortable chair at the table set aside for parents. Here you can unwind while the president presides over Telling The News.

• Your only need for action comes if someone in a station is making a real disturbance. Then all you need say is, "Bailiff, take five points off South Station. Someone in that station is fooling around and not paying attention." This is usually all that is needed to get the attention of all the stations and alerts potential problem makers to stop what they are doing.

• Do make a conscious decision to relax physically. If you have never taken a course in relaxation consider getting one of the many books or tapes available to learn relaxation techniques. With practice you can notice a real difference in only three or four minutes.

In this chapter you have discovered how important it is to nourish your mental, emotional and physical well-being and how you can make the time to do this.

In the next chapter, you will discover how essential it is to hold daily Class Meetings with your students.

CHAPTER 10

CLASS MEETING

10

Class Meeting

*I*n order to teach in a successful HIP classroom, you need to arrange a time to listen to the complaints which frequently arise in the room.

Paul cannot find the new baseball glove he brought to school for Telling the News. He tells his teacher he saw Mike, a classmate, with a glove exactly like his at recess.

Phil complains to his teacher that while playing soccer, Doug, a fellow student, deliberately kicked him.

Amy says to her teacher, "Mark threw food across the table at me in the cafeteria and it's the third time this week."

HELP! CLASS MEETING NEEDED HERE

What is a Class Meeting? Who is the leader? When should a Class Meeting be held?

A Class Meeting is a carefully controlled, teacher-directed activity. The goals for the meeting may vary from grade level to grade level. For the lower grades, Class Meeting is a time when children can get their gripes out in the open. Most of the time, their complaints center around the way they are treated by fellow classmates, and students at this age are quick to bring up problems involving other classmates.

In the intermediate grades, the Class Meeting is a problem solving time when students can feel free to discuss anything from room arrangement to dislike of a class activity as well as an opportunity to express feelings.

HIP TIP In the upper grades, use an agenda which can be written on the chalkboard just before the meeting. Have students write their problems or questions on paper and drop the slips into a designated box. Students who are shy might choose not to have their names on the paper. Just having the teacher bring up the problem and allowing class time for an open discussion can be sufficient.

Students in the HIP program are aware they are not to tattle, yet some always will. The teacher must quietly, but firmly say, "Bring it up at Class Meeting later today."

When writing the rules on Mondays, take the time to specifically talk about "Reporting" only. Remind the class when someone has been hurt, or is ill, you need to know. All other complaints will be addressed at Class Meetings.

The timing of the Class Meeting is important. If at all possible, conduct it during the last 20 minutes of the day. If your class is on the early-late reading schedule, hold the meeting just before early students go home. Departure provides a natural ending to the meeting.

Normally, allow 15 minutes for Class Meeting. If more problems than usual arise during a particular day, allow extra time.

HOW TO CONDUCT A CLASS MEETING

Begin by ringing the bell or alerting the students in some way that Class Meeting will begin in a few minutes. Students need to clear their desks and be sitting quietly before the meeting begins so that all students can be heard, even those with soft voices.

HIP TIP If students are slow to settle down for Class Meeting, find one station ready to begin. Example: If it is West Station say, "West, you are doing great. Your station is quiet and ready for Class Meeting. You've just earned 10 points." This will get the other stations' attention in a hurry.

Sit at the Chairman of the Board table. The bailiff should be sitting near the Honor Point chart and at your directions will take off points for misbehaving students.

Ask the bailiff which station is ahead. If it is South Station, as an example, say, "Does anyone in South Station have a compliment to share in Class Meeting today?" Then ask for problems which need to be discussed.

Have pencil and paper available and take brief notes on students' names, a few words describing the problem, and stations involved.

HIP TIP Provide yourself with a timer. If you expect the Class Meeting to last about 20 minutes, set the timer to ring in 15 minutes. This will alert you, if you're in the midst of settling a major problem, that it is time to end the meeting. Always allow an extra few minutes after the timer rings to get the students ready and out the door.

Here's a typical example of a Class Meeting problem: Amy is unhappy, as we saw, because someone threw food at her in the cafeteria. Amy is not permitted to give the offending student's name, rather, the food thrower is first given the opportunity to admit to the act.

Amy raises her hand and when Mrs. Smith recognizes her, she stands and explains that someone in North Station threw food at her.

Mrs. Smith: "North Station, Amy tells me that someone in

your station was breaking a cafeteria rule by throwing food today. Will that someone please stand up?"

Sometimes the student involved will stand immediately, but not often. Wait a few moments to see if someone will stand. Then look at Amy and say, "Will you tell me who threw food at you today?"

Amy: "Mark did. It's the third time this week and I told him I was going to bring it up at Class Meeting today."

Mrs. Smith: "How did it make you feel, Amy, to have Mark throw food at you?"

Amy: "I felt really sad 'cause he messed up my new blouse and sort of mad, too, 'cause he got food in my hair."

Mrs. Smith: "Mark, please stand. Did you throw food at Amy this week?"

Mark: "Yes."

Tell Mark how disappointed you are in his behavior and explain how he made Amy feel bad. Then ask him to apologize to Amy. Wait a moment for Mark to look at Amy and say, "I'm sorry."

The majority of students are satisfied when someone apologizes for a minor offense but with more serious incidents an apology isn't enough.

HIP TIP I had one student, in particular, who refused to apologize to anyone in the classroom. I could have put the Class Meeting on "hold" till Christmas and the kid still would refuse to say, "I'm sorry." I had the class take a vote about what we should do with Ron. They voted that he had to walk the Perimeter the next day and miss P.E. Frequently this was enough to make him say the magic words. But, other days he chose to walk the Perimeter. I had a parent conference with his mother and she said, "The kid has been stubborn since the day he was born." I then understood. This tip shows that not all problems will be solved.

STUDENTS WHO HURT OTHERS

When students hit, kick and threaten to beat up other students, you must take a firmer approach. The offending student needs to understand that he, or she, has done something very serious and will be held personally responsible.

In cases where students hurt others it works well to ask the injured students to suggest some form of punishment for the offender. With the Perimeter rule built into the HIP system, this is usually the punishment suggested and works well.

As these more serious issues arise, it is wise to have the class vote on what should be done as punishment. The student creating the problem must be made to realize that his, or her, behavior is wrong and is unacceptable to the classroom.

Here is an example: If one of your students grabs the yard stick off the chalk tray and hits the kid next to him say, "Stephen, why did you hit Ralph and put yourself on the Perimeter?"

Between student peer pressure and your words, these misbehaving students should become fully aware that they are doing unacceptable acts which must stop.

HIP TIP If you have a student who continually creates a problem getting in line, or while in line, talk with the student and see where he or she would like to stand in line each day. Example: If the student says, "I want to be the second one in line," ask the class to vote on this request. Having the student assigned to a particular place reduces tardiness and fooling around in line, especially if they get to be in the front of the line next to the Class President.

However, some students will still refuse to cooperate in line, out of line or anywhere. This is when more serious consequences are needed.

THE NEXT STEP: SOS

Not only must you be concerned with the misbehaving students in your classroom, but you must also zero in on each station's overall morale. Stations, especially those with one or two severe discipline problem students, can quickly become discouraged over constant loss of points. They may fear never having the opportunity to take part in the Monday Jobs meeting.

To address this problem, you must speak to the misbehaving student, saying "if you choose to misbehave and lose points for your station, you will become a "student-out-of-station" (SOS). Then tell the class that if any student loses three points during the week, he or she will be placed "out-of-station."

Explain that any student who *chooses* to lose three points for the station will have his or her name placed on the board with SOS beside it. Then tell the class that being "out-of-station" means that student will be the last one in line that day for recess, lunch and P.E. Even if the station is ahead and goes out first, any SOS students will be the last to leave the room.

After the class has filed outside for recess, for example, you may wish to take your time getting your things together before leaving the room. This will further emphasize the point that good behavior pays off and poor behavior does not.

While discussing the SOS sequence, tell the class that in order for students listed as SOS to get back into the station they must earn five points. Only then, may they erase their name from the chalkboard and again become part of the station with all the rights and privileges of the other students.

Also, emphasize that getting back into the station might take time. For example: Randy, one of my students, was "out-of-station" before early recess one morning. Soon he was able to earn back extra points for his station and the extra points were noted in the total for North Station where he was seated. Also, the extra points were placed next to his name on the chalkboard. He finally earned three points for this station by afternoon. But after recess, he got into trouble in his station and lost a point. The point was not removed from his station's total but it was noted after his name. He had to work hard the remainder of the day to earn back the lost point and the additional three so he could remain "in station."

IF SOS DOESN'T WORK

However, some students in your class will continue to engage in hurtful actions against others no matter how many times they walk the Perimeter and how many times they've been placed on SOS. You should keep an anecdotal record on these students. For these very few pupils, it is sometimes necessary to go outside the classroom for help. Talk it over with the principal and the parents and, if a school counselor is available, arrange a meeting to discuss the problem.

At times, after digging deeper into the issue you will find major changes or ongoing problems in the home, which create upsets for the student that carry over into the classroom.

Putting such students on behavior contracts can work well if the parents will cooperate with you. If they refuse, you as the teacher and the peer pressure from the stations can still have an influence upon the particular student.

To set up daily contracts, meet with both student and parents, if possible, and discuss the need for the contract and exactly what it is. Either you or the student takes a three by five card and puts the student's name and the date at the top of the card. To make the whole process easier make a month's worth of cards. Give the student a card at the end of each day. By prearrangement with the parents, your signature and a happy face means a good day. Your signature with a huge "X" means a bad day.

HIP TIP Hide the cards in a safe place. (I've had problem students take them from my desk, make a happy face and dash for home.)

Encourage parents to discover something the child really wants and to tell the student how many cards equal the promised gift. One of my students loved to ride his mini-bike on weekends. He would shape up in hurry in order to get five good cards so he could ride. If I noticed him getting ready to hit someone, I'd pantomime a big "X" in the air and he would stop at once. I never had to say a word.

Keeping in close touch with the home is important so the student knows that what goes on at school is not a separate part of life. The home pressure, along with yours, can frequently bring about an amazing change in a child's behavior.

As this change begins, suggest positive ways for the class to acknowledge it. Three claps for getting through the day without having to walk the Perimeter or having the class vote to have the student lead the class over to the library instead of the president tells problem students loud and clear that good behavior PAYS OFF.

CLASS MEETINGS BENEFIT ALL STUDENTS

How do Class Meetings help students? Why is it so important to take 20 minutes out of a busy day for another meeting? What does this type of meeting teach students?

First of all, the Class Meeting gives students an open forum to present their story fully before the teacher and the class.

HIP TIP Many students especially in primary grades will come up during the day, complaining that three terrible things happened that they must present at the Class Meeting. However, this would make the Class Meeting much too long. Instead say, "I'm sure all three are important, but you'll have to pick the most important one to bring up." This helps students to gain skills at making decisions.

Another important point and, of extreme interest to the student, is that not only will a problem be heard but retribution of some kind will be meted out. In this process, the students see democracy in action.

Students learn during Class Meetings that their problems are important, that they are valued and their view point carries weight. All of this builds self-esteem into their lives.

Students also quickly learn through Class Meetings, that their bodies are important. That no one has a right to call them vulgar names, to hit or kick them. If this should happen during the day, they can be heard, and respected at the Class Meeting forum, and punishment will be swift for the guilty party.

ROLE OF THE TEACHER IN THE CLASS MEETING

More than anything else the teacher serves as a model of how our judicial system works. Students learn what is right and wrong.

HIP TIP Don't let students stand up in Class Meeting and recite the vulgar names they were called. This can set off a giggling session. Instead, ask the student to come up and whisper the word in your ear. This will take a lot of the emotion out of the incident while letting you determine if the word was really bad or just something silly.

The teacher serves in the role of judge in the classroom and the no-nonsense Class Meeting is highly structured with a rigid format. The very same procedure is followed day after day with the only change being that the station with the most points leads off.

Students see that the teacher/judge listens and sometimes asks for more information from other students involved before making a decision.

The teacher should certainly let feelings show during Class Meeting. A teacher says in a sad voice, "Brian, I cannot believe you would call Sharon such an unpleasant name. That makes me sad." Students need to hear genuine emotion in a teacher's voice when they misbehave. These emotions can range from a smile to shock to visible distress that anyone in the class would do such a thing. Students need to see how their actions can cause others harm.

On occasion, the teacher invites input from other students and children can produce back-up witnesses, if needed, to prove their point. In other words, the teacher must be willing to take the time to clearly understand what happened.

HIP TIP Frequently Class Meetings tend to drag on. This is why it's vital to hold the meeting at the end of the day. However, when the timer rings some students will yell out, "But, I didn't get my turn." You can observe, "Tomorrow if you work harder, perhaps your station will have the most points and you'll start Class Meeting." However, if someone is very upset you can take the child aside for a moment and listen to the problem. Often, a listening ear is enough and by tomorrow the crisis will be forgotten.

In this chapter you have learned the importance of the Class Meeting for students in a HIP classroom. In the next chapter, you will discover how to motivate students to do their very best in your successful classroom.

CHAPTER 11

REACHING FOR THE STARS

11

Reaching For The Stars

*T*en-year old Becky has an album with over a hundred stickers she earned by memorizing the times table. She loves to show it off at family gatherings.

Mike, a fourth grader, is a Cub Scout. He has worked hard all year to earn his Bear patch which he proudly wears on his uniform.

Laura, a third grader, is determined to get five "A's" on her report card. If she does, her grandparents have promised to buy her a new bike.

The majority of children love to compete for awards, to work toward goals and be winners. Teachers can use this natural drive to encourage students to do their best in school through a simple method which awards daily achievers.

HIP TIP Some students refuse to do their best and do not try to achieve. For these few, you must come up with alternative methods to encourage them to strive to do their best work. Positive praise for a job well done, a three clap by the class when a project is completed and happy notes home can frequently make a difference in the attitude of reluctant learners.

THE STAR CARD SYSTEM

Provide each student in the class with a five by seven-inch card in an unusual color. Do not use white cards as they are more available and some ingenious student will try to duplicate them.

Use colors such as pink, blue, or yellow, if you can find them (again to cut down on duplications) and put each student's name on the top right-hand corner of the card and the words, "Star Card" on the left.

HIP TIP Take a box used for manila folders and cover it with paper such as a vivid green or blue. Take both large and small stars in silver and gold and stick them all over the sides of the box. If you wish to be more dramatic, take glue like Elmers and write "Star Box" on the side. Then sprinkle the glue words with glitter! The students will find the box irresistable to use. This is where the students place a card when they have collected 20 stars.

MAKING THE STAR SYSTEM WORK

At the beginning of the year tell the class that they will be responsible for keeping their cards in their desks. Explain that the only time they should be out is for reading or math or, at your instructions, during certain language periods and on Fridays for the spelling test.

Tell the students that you will come by during reading and math and check their daily work. If they have an "A" paper, you will draw a star on their card.

The stars are also very useful when writing sentences or paragraphs in language. You can determine, depending upon the grade level, how many stars should be given for written sentences or a paragraph.

Students need to know that a sentence such as, "The boy runs," lacks "star quality." The stars can also be used for special occasions when writing on a subject such as "Fire Prevention in the Forest," "Killer Bees In California," or, "The Day My Turtle Died." Students can earn stars by writing thank you notes to a classroom guest speaker, a mother who dropped by with cupcakes, or for thanking the custodian for fixing the lights in the classroom.

OTHER WAYS FOR USING STAR CARDS

Especially if your class is on the early-late reading program, the cards can help to promote good papers, along with independent work habits when you are working with a small group.

Explanation: "Early-late" means that half of your class comes to school for example, at 8:30 each morning. The remainder of the class comes at 9:30. The early people go home first and the late readers stay an additional hour.

When you are working with the small reading group, it is essential that you are not interrupted by the rest of the students. If you have mothers who come to help, or monitors who come in from the upper-grades to supervise, they can also draw a star on the cards of students who had good work and behaved during the reading period.

SPELLING STARS

To encourage students to know their spelling words, give a star to each student who earns an "A" on the Friday spelling test. Also, if you give bonus words as part of the test, such as big words like Halloween, Christmas or months of the year, you may wish to give a star for each of the bonus words spelled correctly.

COUNTING THE STARS

Students are in charge of not only keeping the cards but of keeping a running tally. Tell them that when they get 20 stars they are eligible for a coupon to turn in for a prize. Direct them to put the cards with the number 20 circled on the top of the card into the star box. You can double check their counting later and issue a new card and a coupon. If a student forgets and ends up with 25 stars on a card, draw five stars on the new card.

STAR PRIZES

Each teacher and school must decide how to award prizes. Here are a few suggestions which have worked well:

1. In some HIP classrooms, each Star Card is worth 10 points for the student's station.

2. Hold an assembly once a month and have the students bring their winning coupons. (Some schools call these Winner Assemblies.) At the end of the assembly, the students turn in all winner coupons for a certificate donated by a fast food burger chain in the area. Some convenience stores donate passes for winning students to play video games.

3. At the end of each month, some teachers may choose to take the students with the most star cards out for a burger or hot fudge sundae. (See chapter 12 for ways to raise funds for these "extras" in your classroom.)

4. A principal at one school walks the entire class to the park when they have achieved so many "good behavior points" in the school lunch room. In this case the park is about six blocks from the school and the students work very hard to spend an hour playing.

In this chapter you have learned the importance of challenging students to do and be their very best. Star cards are one way of saying, "Well done. You are a winner!"

In Chapter 12 you'll discover some additional ideas for making your HIP classroom a resounding success.

CHAPTER 12

GOING HIP

12

Going Hip

Now that you've read about the HIP system, perhaps you've decided to join. Here are some additional ideas to help you along the way.

FLEXIBILITY

Although the basic format of the HIP classroom is highly structured, you can and should remain flexible. Example: Some days will be so packed with meeting subject deadlines that you'll glance up at the clock and realize it's almost time for the early group (if you have early/late readers) or the entire class to go home. What then?

Stop and explain to your students there will not be time for a Class Meeting today, but assure them you will hold one tomorrow. Some students will be angry and will let you know how displeased they are. Remind these few, perhaps as they walk out the door, that sometimes it is impossible to fit everything into one day but they will have their day tomorrow. You'll learn that some days can become so hectic there is not time for Telling The News or Tell Time.

Assure students once again they may leave their sharing items on the shelf until tomorrow when both activities will be conducted.

PARENTS' REACTIONS TO THE HIP PROGRAM

Mrs. Carson was the mother of eight-year-old Jessica in my class. She came to see me the week before school opened and asked if she could help me in the classroom. I was ecstatic! One afternoon, during the third week of school, she was sitting in the back of the room grading papers when I rang the bell and announced, "Class Meeting."

She continued to work quietly during the first ten minutes of the meeting. Then I noticed her hand waving in the air at me. After I finished with the station, I called upon her. She said, "I think this meeting is ridiculous! These kids ought to know how to behave themselves. They don't need to be spending their time complaining about others calling them bad names and kicking them."

I briefly explained to her why we had the meeting, thanked her for her input and continued with the Class Meeting.

During the recess break, I took Mrs. Carson to the Faculty Room with me and explained in more detail why we held Class Meetings. Since she had never worked in a classroom, she was not aware of the amount of time spent by students tattling. I told her the meeting provided angry students with a place to let off steam, to resolve differences and to hear offenders say, "I'm sorry." Then I told her with the built-in Class Meeting we could spend the rest of the day doing schoolwork instead of having students constantly pouring out their difficulties with others to the teacher. She understood.

The remaining parents who came into the room to help during the year were thrilled with the HIP classroom management system. One said to me, "My daughter is learning so much this year because she is in a room where there is order and discipline."

Another parent said, "Mark is elated to have been elected Class President. It's done wonders for his self-esteem."

Another father who frequently brought in some of his daughter's pets such as birds, hamsters and fish told me how much he enjoyed coming into the room. "Telling The News gives Kristi a way of not only showing off her pets but draws her out, as well." He particularly liked the parade when he could go around with her, help her show the pets and answer some of the students' questions.

Another day, the principal stopped by to give us a happy report about the class's behavior in the cafeteria. As he was leaving I asked the class to do a three clap to show him how much we appreciated the good news. He smiled and said, "Now I've never seen anything like that before but it is certainly a great idea."

STUDENTS REACTIONS TO HIP

I never told my students they were in a HIP classroom, especially one I was field-testing, but they took to the system right away.

Not all primary classes hold Show and Tell or Telling The News, so my students were pleased that they could bring in special items to share with others. As students carried in bags containing a new toy or a cactus plant or a caterpillar, they would beam. One said to me, "I can hardly wait for Telling The News 'cause I have something very important to show. Look, it's a polywog I caught at the park yesterday."

Others, especially those with mothers who were expecting, would remind me not to forget Tell Time as they wanted to report the latest on the coming BIG event at their house.

Another positive point for HIP is that it provides a method for helping the teacher to get students to cooperate. This is primarily achieved by peer pressure on misbehaving students. Example: Cindy loved to talk. Her mouth was going all the time. By the third week at school, Cindy was daily reminded by the other students in her West Station that they would not let her continue to do this. After repeatedly having points subtracted from her station for her talking and reprimands from station mates, she settled down.

The HIP system also serves as a reminder to students who continually forget their school materials. For a time, at the beginning of the year, some students would leave reading books at home. The forgetful students did not appear to be bothered by this because they would sit next to a friend with a book and chatter. I suggested at Class Meeting that we should decide what should happen to students who forgot reading books.

The class voted that a forgetful student should not participate in P.E. and instead walk the Perimeter the day the book was left at home. Absent-minded students began to remember to bring their books. If they forgot, classmates were quick to remind them as they walked in the door each morning, by saying, "You didn't bring your reader, did you? Remember what we voted on at Class Meeting? You have to walk the Perimeter today." With glee-filled voices students with readers, without my saying one word, served as daily reminders about forgotten books. Soon, almost all of the students were ready to read out of their own book each day.

Another plus for HIP came each Monday. Perhaps the most enjoyable part of the system for students was holding jobs and offices in the classroom. Mondays were eagerly looked forward to as I've mentioned. One student said to me upon entering the class on Monday morning, "Now, don't forget to have the Job Meeting right away 'cause my station got the most points on Friday, right?"

Not only did most of my students enjoy their jobs and being officers in the classroom but here are some notes taken from conversations with parents: "I wanted Cindy to stay home from school today but she said she wanted to come because she is bailiff this week."

Another parent said, "The jobs are certainly teaching my son to be more responsible and I'm all for that."

A parent commenting upon her shy daughter said, "Being president has helped Erin to speak up and to talk more which is something we had been trying to work on with her at home."

Not only were parents thrilled with the program; so was I.

MY REACTIONS TO HIP

I was ready for HIP. I had just completed a most difficult year with a class which was hard to manage. I had pulled out my usual "bag of discipline tricks" gleaned over 20 years but these simply did not do the job.

That summer I spent my time saturating myself with HIP methods. Before school began I made notes on how to begin the first day. These were typed on 5×7 cards which I attached to my Lesson Plans. I then made similar notes for introducing Telling the News and Telling Time, the first Job Meeting and Class Meeting. I studied these notes until I fully understood each step and felt comfortable about introducing them to my students.

This year I was told by other teachers that I had a "good class." There was the usual number of behavior problems in the mix, but I wasn't alone; I was no longer the sole disciplinarian. The system was designed to use peer pressure to bring students into line. I began to initiate the program on a day-by-day basis. Slowly I could see the change in the students. Even some of the more difficult students in the room began to shape up.

Misbehaving students discovered those seated around them did not want them in their station. It was not unusual for students, during Class Meeting, to ask if they could vote a problem student out of their station. Misbehaving students were faced with a choice of obeying the rules or having to move to another station where, often, they were not wanted. I seldom had to say a word because the students themselves got the word out for me. Caution: Do not let students vote others out of their station. Only the teacher moves students.

I no longer was viewed as the "bad guy" in the room, meting out warnings, writing names on the board or keeping students after school. Instead the rules were on the board. Students knew ahead of time what would happen when rules were disobeyed because they understood the consequences of loss of Honor Points for a station and the Perimeter. They also had a good idea that they would have to "face the music" at the Class Meeting.

ANOTHER TEACHER'S REACTION

A teacher from another state was directed to my room to observe one day. After walking about the room, talking with students and asking questions she said to me, "You have a system here that works. I would like to talk with you more about how you run this room." We made arrangements to meet and discuss the HIP system.

FEELING GOOD ABOUT HIP

I strongly believe that feeling good should be part of a teacher's day and that's the way I felt almost every day in my HIP classroom. I looked forward to going to school; the students, I could tell, enjoyed having me there.

Now I'm going to give you some ideas about two important parts of teaching in a HIP room: managing time and money.

TIME MANAGEMENT

One of the first teachers I told about this program protested, "I won't have time to *teach!*"

It might seem so at first, but I found I actually had more time available for productive teaching.

As I've already mentioned, you won't be able to do everything in the HIP system every day. This is fine. But whenever possible, hold your Tell Time. Also, for your own peace of mind, try to hold at least an abbreviated Class Meeting each day. This means: "I only have time to hear an emergency type problem today." Often this is of the nature of a complaint that "Steve is going to beat me up on the way home from school. I'm afraid to leave." This should be addressed at once, not only for the safety of the fearful student but to alert Steve that we are all on to you. So watch out!

It might appear that keeping track of the Honor Point system is time-consuming. Keeping track of points for big items brought to class each morning can be done in five minutes or less. During the rest of the day, stepping to the Honor chart should take only a moment. I sometimes simply add a $+1$ or a -1 by the station in question and change the totals later.

HIP TIP Remember when you are busy helping a student in the back of the room and notice a disturbance in a station you need not leave the student you are helping. Instead, use your bailiff.

On mornings when I'm especially busy, I may not get to the Honor Point chart and change the totals for each station until just before recess or lunch. The same is true in the afternoon. I may not change them again till recess or just before the students go home. But the majority of the time, by student demand, I do keep the total correct. This does not take long. Again, use the upgrading of points as a time to teach math both adding, subtracting, borrowing and carrying.

One of the great joys in the HIP program is not having to direct every activity every minute of the day. This means during Telling The News and Tell Time I have my own private "Time Out" while the president conducts these activities. It is true that some "Time Out" periods I must work on my register or talk with a parent. But the class moves forward very well without my presence in the front of the room. It is my time to breathe deeply, to regroup, to relax.

Another bonus is I no longer have to keep misbehaving students after school. The system takes care of these problem students through the use of subtracting points from their station. This also means an immediate reprimand, as mentioned, from station mates for "doing this to us." And, if this peer pressure does not work, I use the Perimeter to remind the student to "settle down."

This year was very successful for me because the HIP system made me *feel* successful as I walked through each organized day.

MONEY MATTERS

Teachers vary widely in their views on spending their own money for the classroom. Some get by, by "making do." Others, go all out spending money year after year.

In the HIP program, I did spend some money in my classroom. But, I also found ways to help students raise money so we could do a few "extras" each year as pure pleasure or to pay for out-of-town field trips.

Money was spent to provide Hershey bars each Friday for our reading tutors from the intermediate grades, for popcorn for special Friday movies and to take award-winning students to lunch once a month. I also purchased trinkets at a discount store and kept these in a grab bag as prizes for consecutive numbers.

But you do not have to pay for these extras. Here are several teacher-tested ideas for raising money for your classroom projects:

CUPCAKE SALES — Have a parent head up the sale. Give her the names of others you think might be willing to work. Ask each parent in your class to bake two dozen cupcakes. If some cannot, they should know that you understand and it will not in anyway reflect on their child. Other mothers frequently are willing to bake additional cupcakes.

Advertise the sale for at least one week previous to the big day. Have your students design and paint colorful posters to place all around the school telling about the sale.

HIP TIP If you are teaching in the lower grades, you won't have a student old enough to design posters. Instead, ask an intermediate teacher to suggest a few talented art students in their room. Provide the students with paper, colored pens and your ideas for the poster. Usually, students are thrilled to see their work with signature on the school building and they will not only do the posters but hang them as well.

You and your students can help by designing and wearing a sandwich board advertising the sale. It should be worn before school, to meet all incoming buses and on recess and lunch hour. Do this for at least three days before the sale.

Ask one mother to bring in her cupcakes the day before the sale making them extra tempting. Wear the sandwich board and carry the "advertising" cupcakes on a tray around the playground with some of your students accompanying you and sing-song, "Chocolate, Devils Food, Banana cupcakes on sale tomorrow. Bring your money!" Heads will turn and wallets will open for your cause.

Ask your office if they would be willing to send home a notice by each student to the parents telling them the name of the classroom putting on the sale, the reason, the day and the cost of each cupcake. This is especially important information for kindergarten students to get home.

HIP TIP One teacher raised **$340** holding a three-hour cupcake sale. Not only did parents help at a large table for students wishing to purchase any number of cupcakes but one parent was in charge of a small table located near the bus stop with a sign which read FAST CUPCAKES! ONE ONLY. This arrangement permitted students to get faster service and in many cases not miss the bus.

NEWSPAPERS — Waste paper recycling dealers are in the business of collecting LARGE amounts of newspapers. Take advantage of this. Ask a father in your room to head up the paper collecting campaign. Advertise widely in the community for at least one month prior to the Saturday collection date.

The typical paper dealer will provide you with a locked metal box similar in size to the ones found on construction sites. The box is delivered on a Friday to your school. On Saturday have your students load up their wagons, their parents' cars and trucks with newspapers collected from their neighborhoods.

On the designated Saturday the papers are taken to the school site and the father in charge unlocks the metal box and loads in the paper. The dealer will come back on Monday and pick up the container, weigh it and pay your class. The price will vary from city to city so call your local waste paper recycling dealer for prices.

COLLECTING ALUMINUM CANS — Another way to make extra money is to have your students collect aluminum cans. Keep a large plastic lined garbage can in the back of your room. Encourage your students to smash the cans before bringing them into the classroom. Another drawing card is to have students bring in the cans and as soon as the barrel is full, have a "smashing party" out on the playground. You get the job done and kids love the action. It will also help you to get the barrel filled up faster. Caution: Before doing this, show your students how to "smash" the cans correctly so no one gets hurt. Recycling companies pay different amounts per pound from city to city. Again call your local dealer to get the exact price. Ask a parent to be in charge of turning the cans in when you have a good collection.

One teacher collects enough over a few months to make $15 towards class projects. Give it a try.

SATURDAY FILMS — Here is an idea which can bring in a large amount of money in a few hours. Consider ordering a special film such as "Charlotte's Web," along with a cartoon to show in your multipurpose hall on a Saturday morning.

Example: Outstanding films can be ordered from Far West Films, Inc. in San Francisco. Call (415) 565-3000. Again, advertise widely for at least a week or two before the film showing. Enlist parents to be in charge of donating popcorn, Kool Aid, and hot dogs for the intermission. Not only do you charge each child a fee for seeing the movie, you also make money on the concessions. One teacher made over $300 doing this on a single Saturday morning.

These are certainly not the only ways of raising money for your classroom, but these suggestions may trigger some ideas of your own such as a class newspaper to sell to parents and other students.

Caution: I would discourage students from going door-to-door today selling candy, candles or other items.

CONCLUSION

Now you've been introduced to the HIP system. You may wish to try out the entire package or only parts of it. Only you know what will work best in your classroom. No management system is the "perfect one" for everyone.

If you do choose to use the HIP system, feel free to change it to fit your own particular classroom and students. Then enjoy a most successful school year.

CHAPTER 13

QUESTIONS AND ANSWERS

13

Questions And Answers

GENERAL QUESTIONS

Q. Isn't this just one more way to use Behavior Modification in the classroom?

A. First of all, let's define Behavior Modification. It is based upon the learning theory which rewards good behavior and punishes poor behavior in the belief that rewarded behavior will increase while punished behavior will decrease.

Technically HIP could be considered Behavior Modification, but with a twist! At times, one student is rewarded or punished, as the case may be. However, the central focus of this system is to change the behavior of individual students through the use of peer pressure. Rather than the teacher spending time disciplining an individual student for breaking classroom rules, the desired behavior change is made through the use of peer pressure within each station thus freeing the teacher to do what he or she does best — teach!

Q. I think the HIP plan sounds great but I'm not sure my principal would go along with it. How could I approach him so he will agree to let me use the system?

A. Some schools use only one discipline program and you may not be free to change it. However, I would go to the principal and tell him you want to change to HIP as soon as possible. Also, I would let him read the HIP book. Even if he is not open to the idea this year, let him know that you wish to become a HIP classroom next year. You might even offer to be a test room for the school. Most principals are open to suggestions, especially those which have been field tested with proven results.

Q. I teach sixth graders. I don't think my students would buy into the Monday jobs as a payoff for following the rules in the classroom. What do you suggest?

A. Here are two suggestions from fifth and sixth grade teachers. One fifth grade teacher uses a weekly auction to improve classroom discipline. He collects coupons from local burger shops plus used games and other white elephants from friends. The students also bring in items they wish to put in the auction. When students line up correctly, behave in class and obey classroom rules he pays them each a specific amount of play money to be used at the weekly auction. The students look forward to this period each week and work hard for the opportunity to bid on favorite items.

Be aware that problems do arise even when using play money. Students may steal from each other, so each person is urged to take the money home until the day of the auction. A solution might be to provide a bank with officers chosen from the classroom to alleviate the problem. Hint: The idea of using play money at the intermediate level is something you should consider. It motivates students to work hard, mind rules and keep up homework.

Another teacher uses the point system but instead of Monday jobs, she has her sixth graders elect certain field trips — most out of town. By earning points, students can go on the trips they select. Her particular school has additional funding which helps defray some costs. If your school does not have extra funding, read Chapter 12 for ways you can raise money to take your class on special outings.

PARENTS IN THE CLASSROOM

Q. I have 31 students this year in my second grade classroom and no teacher's aide. I can't seem to get parents to help. What can I do?
A. Ideally, you should begin the first day of school by asking for help. Also, as the year progresses, continue to recruit parents. In the beginning, send home a general informational note introducing yourself, the classroom schedule and your needs. At the bottom of the sheet, have a coupon designed as a simple check-off sheet for parents. Tell your students you will give each student in a station ten points for returning the coupon.

Here is an example:
PLEASE CLIP AND RETURN TO MRS. WILLIAMSON
BY FRIDAY

Mrs. Williamson: I'm willing to help in the classroom. I've circled the days I can come and I have checked in the box the time I can come.
(Circle days you can help)
Monday   Tuesday   Wednesday   Thursday   Friday
(Check in box the time you can come)
☐ 8:30 to 9:30 for Reading
☐ 9:30 to 10:30 for Language
☐ 10:30 to 11:30 for Math
☐ 12:45 to 1:30 on Fridays for Art
☐ Other
I'm not able to help in the classroom but I'm willing to do the following:
☐ Go on field trips
☐ Grade papers at home
☐ Prepare art lessons
☐ Be a classroom speaker
☐ Other_____

☐ I have special hobbies I could share with the class. Here are some ideas: model airplanes, raise birds, write poetry, kite making, musical instruments.

Fathers are also welcome to take part in our classroom. In the past I've had fathers talk to us about fishing, birds and go with us on field trips.

Your name:_____

When the coupons come in, look them over and make a tally sheet which should be posted on your personal bulletin board or kept in a folder at your desk for easy referral.

Q. How can I best use these offers of help?
A. Be prompt to send notes home to the parents emphasizing your appreciation that they are going to help you during the year.

For parents willing to work at home, let them know you will try to give them at least three days' notice before sending materials. This way you do not drop work into parents' laps unexpectedly.

For those coming to work in the school, send a note verifying their schedule and let them know you are looking forward to having them work in the classroom with you.

It is imperative you preplan their work. I find making lesson plans for my parents is essential to a smooth running room. Example: Mrs. R. comes into my classroom each Monday at 9:30 and stays for two hours. She does a variety of jobs such as preparing bulletin boards and putting them up each month, working on ongoing art projects and helping me when I work with large groups of students.

I plan ahead each week for her Monday visit and I have a spot where I leave her lesson plans. If I'm busy, she waves and goes to the shelf, reads her work plans for the morning and begins.

Here is an example of a recent Monday: The plans explained that she would be respraying 33 small chalkboards. The note indicated where she would find the necessary supplies and which students would help her. She is very efficient, works quickly and does a fantastic job for me.

Q. How can I best show my appreciation?
A. In order to keep parents coming into my room on a weekly basis (and, at times, some fall by the wayside) I go out of my way to make them feel welcome, important and most of all needed.

It is essential to be a good hostess to your parent helpers. I see my parents as guests in my classroom and I treat them as the very special people they are. Frequently, when they complete a project, I have the class stand and do a three clap to show our classroom appreciation for their efforts.

In addition, on the back counter, near the sink, I have a pretty tray for visitors to use. On it I keep colorful coffee mugs, a basket filled with herbal tea bags, a jar of instant coffee and a small hot pot for heating water. During recess I often encourage the parents to stay in the room with me and relax while we share a cup of tea. (Check to be sure your local fire department will allow you to have a hot pot in the classroom).

At other times, if I do not have duty, I take them into the faculty lounge where I proudly introduce them to the other teachers and provide them with coffee.

In the spring I plan a luncheon held either in my home or at a restaurant where I treat my parent helpers to lunch. Here we can enjoy socializing in a relaxed manner as opposed to the often hectic working schedule in the classroom. We can laugh together and, in general, enjoy an afternoon not as teacher and parents but as friend with friend.

SPECIAL PROBLEMS WITH STUDENTS

Q. I have a hyperactive boy in my fifth grade room. The students complain about his singing, burping and talking in class. He is driving me crazy. What can I do?
A. Set up your room according to the HIP model. Reread Chapter 10 — Class Meeting. Follow the instructions there for dealing with

difficult students.

If the behavior still does not change, I recommend Dr. Paul Wood's book, *How To Get Your Children To Do What You Want Them To Do.* After I had used the HIP treatment, including SOS, Student Out Of Station, with limited results with a boy similar to yours, I read Dr. Wood's book. I found there what I needed to do and how to demand in a loud, firm, no nonsense voice a specific behavior with this student. In Chapter One, "Saying What You Mean — Meaning What You Say," Dr. Wood discusses how to make students behave. He explains that it is crucial to begin by stating the demand in unambiguous terms. He states that the student must really know that you mean what you say. You must not *ask* the student to do something, nor *wish* the student would do something but *tell* the student what you expect. Students know from your voice, your actions and your body language when you really mean what you say.

I was also interested in Dr. Wood's theory that children are not hyperactive, only filled with anxiety — often as a result of problems in the home environment. Dr. Wood, a Los Angeles psychiatrist, describes how a teacher, by demanding specific behavior, can release the anxiety in the child and the student can begin to function more effectively in the classroom. See Appendix-Resources for information on how you may purchase this book and also the companion tapes.

Q. I have several students this year who live in single parent homes and that parent doesn't seem to care whether they behave or not in the classroom. I get no backing from them. What can I do?
A. I have had students come to me from single parent homes who misbehaved and students from homes with both parents and these students also misbehaved. No matter what the home circumstances are, we teachers must set our own standards, enforce them and demand that students behave. We can do this even if we have no parental support. Remember this year you are the second most important person in this student's life next to the parent. Arrange your room to function as a HIP classroom. I would have a private conference with the student and state clearly that the student is part

of the room and *will behave.*

You could also discuss the problem in a Class Meeting. If the other students agree, the youngster could be placed on a contract and on any day when the young person does not lose points for the station, the station would receive a bonus of a specific amount of points (for example 20 points). I would set limits on the contract — like one full month. In the Class Meeting, it would be helpful to let the other stations know that, at a later date, this student might be moved into their station so it is vital that they also encourage the student to behave.

Q. I have a ten-year-old girl in my classroom who is constantly demanding my attention. Within the first five minutes she is in the classroom, she comes up to me at least three times either telling me "home stories" or asking questions about, for example, where she can find a red crayon. She knows perfectly well where they are. How can I get her to be less demanding of my time and attention?

A. I've had similar situations in my classroom. Troy, (not his real name) talks most of the day in my classroom. I've noted that he is a very nervous child. From his records, this has been a continuing problem for him in school. I have had the school counselor interview Troy and he noted the same behavior. Here are the steps I'm taking:

1. I met privately with Troy and we discussed his need to talk to me throughout the day — often in the middle of a lesson I'm teaching. We agreed that some questions were important because they had to do with his seatwork. However, I also made it very clear that when he could control his need to talk to me and to others, he would have more time to listen, get directions and do his seatwork — so he would not have homework each night. We agreed together that he could come up to me seven times a day and either ask or tell me something. He understands that he should pick out the seven most important things he needs to say to me. However, he cannot come up in the middle of a lesson.

2. Each morning I write a small contract on the chalkboard with his name and numbers from one to seven. Each time he comes up, I "x" out the appropriate number.

3. On one of his daily visits, I reminded him how important his questions are, and I'm pleased with how selective he has become in picking out the most important ones to discuss.

Result: Troy recently came to me and said, "I'm doing better, aren't I?" I was pleased to let him know that the day before he needed to use only five of his contract numbers with me and perhaps the following week we should go for five talking times each day. He agreed to try.

Caution: The teacher needs to mark off the numbers. At first I felt Troy should do this. Then I noticed it became a game of running up, talking to me, then dashing over in front of the class and making a big production of finding an eraser and very slowly erasing a tiny number.

Q. I have an unusually high number of active students in my third grade class this year. They have trouble sitting for very long in the classroom doing seatwork. What can I do to settle them down?

A. The physical education program we use in our classroom is a natural for burning off excess energy. In order to add zest to my program, I've purchased jump ropes and hoops for each student. Also, I was able to buy a large parachute from a surplus store to use as a group activity. (Check with your principal before buying the parachute to see if it must be sprayed with fire retardent and then kept secure in a metal can in the classroom so students will not use it as a tent and suffocate themselves). Here is how I sometimes use the jump ropes: after an unusually long math lesson the students frequently become very fidgety. I hand them each a jump rope and we go outside and we do easy warm up exercises for a few minutes. Then we jump "hot peppers" for another minute or so. Later, I ask the students to line up at one end of the blacktop with their ropes ready. I then give a signal and they skip rope down to the end of the blacktop. After a long drink, they return to the classroom and are ready to settle down again. All of this took us less than ten minutes to accomplish. For additional ideas on physical activities see the Appendix-Resource pages in the back of this book.

Here is a final question of importance not only to new teachers but, at times, to each of us.

Q. This is my first year of teaching and I feel so ineffective. How can HIP help me become the strong teacher I dreamed I would be?

A. The HIP system was designed to make you, the teacher, a take-charge person. As Chairman of the Board, you are in charge, but you may need to practice enhancing your self-image as an effective teacher. An excellent way is through affirmations. An affirmation is simply a strong positive statement which you repeat to yourself. Make your own affirmations and put them on cards to look at each morning or make affirmation tapes to listen to while driving to school each morning. Here are some examples:

- I am a take-charge teacher.
- Students are eager to learn what I have to share.
- I am a gifted teacher who cares about my students.
- My students see me as a positive teacher.
- I am confident, serene and happy today.

Affirmations must be written in a positive manner; never use the word *don't*. For instance, instead of saying, "Misbehaving students don't get me down," say, "I competently and calmly deal with misbehaving students."

Buy similar tapes which will help you to become the strong teacher you dreamed of in college. In the Appendix-Resource section you will find information on where to obtain positive tapes to help you become a successful teacher.

APPENDIX

Resources

BOOKS
1. *Assertive Discipline* by Lee Canter. This book, first published in 1976, is basically a guidebook for teachers on how to take charge of discipline in the classroom. Many schools follow Canter's discipline program.

To prepare for writing the book, Canter and his associates visited hundreds of successful classrooms to discover what these teachers did which promoted good classroom discipline. From his research, came this now-famous discipline book which has made such a change in thousands of classrooms across the land.

Since publishing the book, he has also written several complementary workbooks.

For more information contact:
Canter and Associates Inc.
P.O. Box 64517
Los Angeles, CA 90064

2.   *Our Classroom* by Chick Moorman and Dee Dishon. These former school teachers have formed their own company, The Institute for Personal Power, and today are involved in educational consulting and training throughout the United States and Europe.

Dishon and Moorman visited a number of schools before writing the book to view positive methods going on in successful classrooms. The resulting book, subtitled *We Can Learn Together,* tells the reader how to set up a classroom where learning is shared by teacher and student.

For more information contact:
Institute for Personal Power
P.O. Box 68
Portage, MI 49081

3.   *How to Get Children to Do What You Want Them to Do* by Paul Wood. Here is a book of ideas for teachers on how to get students to cooperate, to do their work and to behave. The book is filled with examples from Dr. Wood's practice in child psychiatry in Los Angeles. I strongly recommend this book for teachers working with students with difficult behavior problems.

For more information contact:
Dr. Paul Wood
18800 Main Street, Suite 207
Huntington Beach, CA 92648

4.   *Dare To Discipline* by Dr. James Dobson. Dr. Dobson is a Professor of Pediatrics at the University of Southern California. His book was first published in 1970 but is still available today after many additional printings. It is aimed at parents and teachers who must guide and mold the next generation.

Within the seven chapters, Dr. Dobson leads the reader along a systematic pathway showing how to direct a child toward self-discipline and responsibility.

Chapter 3 titled "Discipline in the Classroom" will be of particular interest to teachers.

For more information contact:
    Bantam Books, Inc.
    666 Fifth Avenue
    New York, N.Y. 10019

5. *Awesome Elementary School Physical Education Activities* by Cliff Carnes. Carnes has been an educator for 20 years. He has been a classroom teacher in the intermediate grades, taught Special Education and has been a school Physical Education Specialist for Grades K-6 for five years.

This book is written in easy-to-read fashion with clear diagrams showing how to teach an assortment of physical education activities to students.

In addition, Carnes offers other materials such as task cards for teaching jump rope activities to students and individual P.E. activity task cards.

For more information contact:
    The Education Company
    3949 Linus Way
    Carmichael, CA 95608

TAPES
1. *May The Force Be With You* by Chick Moorman.

These two tapes are filled with strategies on how to win at teaching. Moorman, formerly a junior high teacher, now with Dee Dishon, co-director of The Institute for Personal Power, is a sought-after speaker and lecturer for teachers.

On the tapes he discusses what winning teachers need to do to be successful, positive, and happy people.

He moves from telling teachers how to be successful in their personal lives to showing how they can help their students be happy, productive and positive in the classroom.

For more information contact:
    The Institute for Personal Power
    P.O. Box 68
    Portage, MI 49081

2. *Understanding Stress and Learning to Relax* by Paul Wood.

Dr. Wood, a child and family psychiatrist from Los Angeles, is heard in this tape addressing a group of teachers regarding the management of stress in their lives.

At the outset, he is quick to say "that none of us will ever hold a job that is not in some way stressful."

He also gives techniques which teachers can use in the classroom to quiet and calm their students on a daily basis.

On the flip side of the tape, Dr. Wood takes the listener, step-by-step, through a process which achieves quiet and calmness.

For more information contact:

Dr. Paul Wood
18800 Main Street, Suite 207
Huntington Beach, CA 92648

3. *How to Get Your Children to Do What You Want Them to Do* by Paul Wood.

On these two tapes, Dr. Wood speaks to a group of parents. However, the material on the tapes also addresses a teacher's problems in the classroom getting students to behave. He gives the example of one boy who refused to go to school. Under Dr. Wood's directions, the mother told her son he *would* go to school. Then, the mother took a week off from work and accompanied the boy to each class. This technique worked. The student, on his own, continued and graduated.

He also describes a situation where a child was a behavior problem at home, at school and in public. When it became impossible for the parents to take the child out in public, they sought Dr. Wood's help. Again, under his directions, following definite guidelines, the parents began to work with the boy. Within a short time, the boy was cooperating and the household returned to normal. The step-by-step techniques listed in both these cases can most certainly be helpful to teachers in the classroom to make students behave.

I recommend this tape very highly if you are dealing with students with severe behavior problems. The tape further develops Dr. Wood's book by the same name.

For more information contact:
    Dr. Paul Wood
    18800 Main Street, Suite 207
    Huntington Beach, CA 92648

124   *Notes:*

ORDER FORM

Dynamic Teaching Company
2247 Palmwood Court
Rancho Cordova, CA 95670 USA
Telephone (916) 638-1136

Please send me Bonnie Williamson's book: *H.I.P. TIPS, How To Organize And Run A Successful Classroom: A Guide For Elementary Teachers.*

_____copies of the book at $9.95 each.

_____For five or more copies deduct 10%.

_____I would like to be notified when *A First Year Teacher's Guidebook To Success* is available.

_____I would like to be notified when *101 Ways To Put Pizazz Into Your Teaching* is available.

_____I would be interested in attending a H.I.P. TIPS workshop.

Name

Address

City   State   Zip

CA Residents		**Out of State**	
Price	$9.95	Price	$9.95
Tax	.60	Shipping	1.00
Shipping	1.00		
Total	$11.55	Total	$10.95

Shipping: Add 25¢ for each additional book.

ORDER FORM

Dynamic Teaching Company
2247 Palmwood Court
Rancho Cordova, CA 95670 USA
Telephone (916) 638-1136

Please send me Bonnie Williamson's book: *H.I.P. TIPS, How To Organize And Run A Successful Classroom: A Guide For Elementary Teachers.*

_____copies of the book at $9.95 each.

_____For five or more copies deduct 10%.

_____I would like to be notified when *A First Year Teacher's Guidebook To Success* is available.

_____I would like to be notified when *101 Ways To Put Pizazz Into Your Teaching* is available.

_____I would be interested in attending a H.I.P. TIPS workshop.

Name

Address

City   State   Zip

CA Residents		**Out of State**	
Price	$9.95	Price	$9.95
Tax	.60	Shipping	1.00
Shipping	1.00		
Total	$11.55	Total	$10.95

Shipping: Add 25¢ for each additional book.